Till Death Do Us Part:

How the Church Should Respond to Domestic Violence

Mark Hunter

authorHOUSE®

AuthorHouse™
1663 Liberty Drive, Suite 200
Bloomington, IN 47403
www.authorhouse.com
Phone: 1-800-839-8640

First published by AuthorHouse 11/22/2008

ISBN: 978-1-4389-3103-6 (sc)

Printed in the United States of America
Bloomington, Indiana

This book is printed on acid-free paper.

Scripture quotations marked (NIV) are taken from the *Holy Bible: New International Version*. NIV®. Copyright © 1973, 1978, 1984 by International Bible Society. Used by permission. All rights reserved.

The "NIV" and "New International Version" trademarks are registered in the United States Patent and Trademark Office by International Bible Society. Use of either trademark requires permission of International Bible Society.

Scripture quotations marked (NKJV) are taken from the New King James Version. Copyright © 1979, 1980, 1982 by Thomas Nelson, Inc. Used by permission. All rights reserved.

Scripture quotations marked (THE MESSAGE) are from *The Message*. Copyright © by Eugene H. Peterson 1993, 1994, 1995. Used by permission.

Scripture quotations marked (KJV) are taken from the King James Version.

Author's note: This book will be discussing Wisconsin law and laws vary greatly from state to state. Crimes may have different names and what might be a felony in Wisconsin may be a misdemeanor somewhere else. No portion of this book is legal advice. This book is intended to explain the dynamics of domestic violence and to help people intervene in positive and worthwhile ways.

This book is dedicated to the victims of domestic violence/sexual assault and to the men and women who work to end violence.

Table of Contents

Chapter One

Understanding Abuse

THEN DAVID MOVED DOWN INTO the Desert of Maon. A certain man in Maon, who had property there at Carmel, was very wealthy. He had a thousand goats and three thousand sheep, which he was shearing in Carmel. His name was Nabal and his wife's name was Abigail. She was an intelligent and beautiful woman, but her husband, a Calebite, was surly and mean in his dealings.

While David was in the desert, he heard that Nabal was shearing sheep. So he sent ten young men and said to them, "Go up to Nabal at Carmel and greet him in my name. Say to him: 'Long life to you! Good health to you and your household! And good health to all that is yours!

"'Now I hear that it is sheep shearing time. When your shepherds were with us, we did not mistreat them, and the whole time they were at Carmel nothing of theirs was missing. Ask your own servants and they will tell you. Therefore be favorable toward my young men, since we come to a festive time. Please give your servants and your son David whatever you can find for them.'"

When David's men arrived, they gave Nabal this message in David's name. Then they waited. Nabal answered David's servants, "Who is this David? Who is this son of Jesse? Many servants are breaking away from their masters these days. Why should I take my bread and water, and meat I have slaughtered for my shearers, and give it to men coming from who knows where?"

David's men turned around and went back. When they arrived, they reported every word. David said to his men, "Put on your swords!" So they put on their swords, and David put on his. About four hundred men went up with David, while two hundred stayed with the supplies.

One of the servants told Nabal's wife Abigail: "David sent messengers from the desert to give our master his greetings, but he hurled insults at them. Yet these men were very good to us. They did not mistreat us, and the whole time we were out in the fields near them nothing was missing. Night and day they were a wall around us all the time we were herding our sheep near them. Now think it over and see what you can do, because disaster is hanging over our master and his whole household. He is such a wicked man that no one can talk to him."

Abigail lost no time. She took two hundred loaves of bread, two skins of wine, five dressed sheep, five seahs (probably about a bushel) of roasted grain, a hundred cakes of raisins and two hundred cakes of pressed figs, and loaded them on donkeys. Then she told her servants, "Go on ahead; I'll follow you." But she did not tell her husband Nabal.

As she came riding her donkey into a mountain ravine, there were David and his men descending toward her and she met them. David had just said, "It's been useless – all my watching over this fellow's property in the desert so that nothing of his was missing. He has paid back evil for good. May God deal with David, be it ever so severely, if by morning I leave alive one male of all who belong to him!"

When Abigail saw David, she quickly got off her donkey and bowed down before David with her face to the ground. She fell at his feet and said: "My lord, let the blame be on me alone. Please let your servant speak to you; hear what your servant has to say. May my lord pay no attention to that wicked man Nabal. He is just like his name – his name is Fool, and folly goes with him. But as for me, your servant, I did not see the men my master sent. Now, since the Lord has kept you, my master from bloodshed and from avenging yourself with your own hands, as surely as the Lord lives and as you live, may your enemies and all who intend to harm my master be like Nabal. And let this gift, which your servant has brought to my master, be given to the men who follow you. Please forgive your servant's offense, for the Lord will certainly make a lasting dynasty for my master, because he fights the Lord's battles. Let no wrong doing be found in you as long as you live. Even though someone is pursuing you to take your life, the life of my master will be bound securely in the bundle of the living by the Lord your God. But the lives of your enemies he will hurl away as from the pocket of a sling. When the Lord has done for my master every good thing he promised concerning him and has appointed him leader over Israel, my master will not have on his conscience the staggering burden of needless bloodshed or of having avenged himself. And when the Lord has brought my master success, remember your servant."

David said to Abigail, "Praise be to the Lord, the God of Israel, who has sent you today to meet me. May you be blessed for your good judgment and for keeping me from bloodshed this day and from avenging myself with my own hands. Otherwise, as surely as the Lord, the God of Israel, lives, who has kept me from harming you, if you had not come quickly to meet me, not one male belonging to Nabal would have been left alive by daybreak."

Then David accepted from her hand what she had brought him and said, "Go home in peace. I have heard your words and granted your request."

When Abigail went to Nabal, he was in the house holding a banquet like that of a king. He was in high spirits and very drunk. So she told him nothing until daybreak. Then in the morning, when Nabal was sober, his wife told him all these things, and his heart failed him and he became like a stone. About ten days later, the Lord struck Nabal and he died.

Well, the story that you just read is verbatim from 1 Samuel 25 (NIV), and we are going to take a look at this story and think about abuse, domestic abuse, domestic violence issues, as I believe that this story speaks a great deal to us about abuse and our response to it. Aside from the account of Cain and Abel in the book of Genesis, this story of Abigail and Nabal, in my opinion, is one of the first documented stories of domestic violence.

So before we dig into the story, let's talk about domestic abuse/violence and understand what it is. I was listening to a radio talk show on a Christian radio station several months back, and the host and co-host were discussing domestic violence and abuse issues. I was very troubled by what I had heard and realized that perhaps the talk show participants just didn't really realize what abuse really was.

One co-host commented, I think more than we realize there are people who are in danger and the lives of the children are also in danger. Could you comment on that?

The second co-host responded, What if you are in an abusive marriage? I think that word "abuse" is greatly misused in our society. So sometimes you're in a tough marriage, where for 29 years you have experienced verbal abuse. That really isn't abuse as much as it is working through a difficult marriage.

The co-hosts go on to discuss how to deal with these issues, and we will look at those ways a few chapters from now, but right now let's try to understand abuse and abusive relationships.

Was Abigail abused? Was Abigail just in a tough marriage? From what we read, Nabal had never physically abused Abigail, that we know of.

Let's examine the story, and first off we will take a look at Nabal. We know that he was a descendant of Caleb, and we know that he was a fool as his name even means fool. The reading said that he was surly. The word surly means cross, having or showing a bad temper; rude and unfriendly according to Webster's American Dictionary. In the King James Version we read that Nabal was "churlish and evil in his doings." We can tell that Nabal thought highly of himself in that he was holding a banquet as that of a king.

Let's look at David. This is the anointed, to be King David, and he is out hiding from Saul in the wilderness and he is one of the first security guards. He and his men kept watch over Nabal's herds and protected his men from others who may harm them or try to steal Nabal's animals. So, when David sent his men, he was hoping to receive payment that he thought he deserved for his services of protection.

How about Abigail? The story described her as beautiful and intelligent. When she hears from one of Nabal's servants that "disaster is hanging over our master and his whole household" she never went to Nabal to discuss the situation. Why not? Can we determine from the words of the servant who pleaded with Abigail, "He is such a wicked man that no one can talk to him," that even Abigail herself would not be able to come to Nabal and feel free to talk to him about this?

Do you know someone like this? Maybe a boss, a co-worker, a parent or sibling? Maybe your own husband or wife? Can you understand what Abigail was feeling? Can you see, just from the few things that we know about Nabal why she would not feel able to talk to Nabal? What do you think would have happened to Abigail had she gone to Nabal and suggested what she thought he should do? What do you think would have happened had Abigail just told Nabal, "Hey, I'm going to put together the first ever catering service and override you and try to stop David." Would Nabal allow her to go against his wishes? Who was she hoping to protect? Nabal? Maybe they have children, the text does not say that they do, but it does say that David was planning to kill Nabal and every male who belongs to him.

Just from examining these questions and your answers to them, is Nabal a controller? Is he a manipulator? Before you can say that Abigail is not an abuse victim, she is merely in a tough marriage, have you ever lived with a controller?

Abigail sets out to deliver all that she has prepared and ends up giving wisdom to the soon-to-be-King – David. We get more insight into Nabal from her comments when she gets off of her donkey and says to David to "pay no attention to that wicked man Nabal. He is just like his name – his name is Fool, and folly goes with him." The King James Version says that Abigail called Nabal "this man of Belial" which means worthless fellow. In the New King James Version we read Abigail saying that Nabal is a "scoundrel" which means a trouble maker.

She reminds David that he fights the Lord's battles, which is a huge contrast to him coming to kill Nabal, just because Nabal refused to give him anything.

Abigail wisely tells David that God has looked out for him, and she says that God will continue to "even though someone is pursuing you to take your life." Isn't that why David was hiding out in the wilderness anyway? Because Saul was hunting him down to destroy David? How many times did David escape being killed by Saul? David had to have been moved by her wise words.

In the same paragraph she said, "But the lives of your enemies he (the Lord) will hurl away as from the pocket of a sling." Wow, did that not remind David of the victory God gave him over Goliath?

She was basically telling David it is wrong to have such anger that you strap on a sword and go kill people. She was telling him that she believed he would be King after Saul's death and she was saying that she didn't want him to do anything that could cast a shadow over his future reign, or keep him from getting the throne, or go against God's will by settling a personal score by killing Nabal and many other innocent people.

David even responds well to her wise counsel and basically agrees that this was a knee-jerk reaction, fueled by anger and revenge. He changes his mind and accepts her gifts.

We get more insight into Nabal when we read that he was holding a banquet, like that of a king. And he was drunk. Had Abigail not met David on his way to slay Nabal, what ability to fend off David and his men would Nabal have had given the condition he was in? Why did Abigail not tell Nabal what she had done while he was drunk? Have you ever confronted a drunk, let alone a mean drunk person, with news that you know that person will take offense to?

As a police officer I have dealt with drunk, mean people, and I can tell you that it is not fun. It is also dangerous and counterproductive. I have met with many abuse victims who said that confronting a mean spouse was bad enough, but if alcohol were involved, they would never deal with that person. The decision to not confront was a matter of survival for them, and I think we can easily see that it was a matter of survival for Abigail.

When Abigail did tell Nabal, it was "in the morning, when Nabal was sober." And the text tells us that after she told him "all these things," that Nabal's heart failed him and he became like a stone, and about ten days later, the Lord struck Nabal and he died.

Nabal had a stroke, was paralyzed and ten days later, he died. Why did this happen to Nabal? From what we know of his character, had he not had a medical condition that stopped him in his tracks, what would have happened to Abigail? Can you imagine the curses he would have had for her? Can you imagine what kind of physical harm she would have been in? I think he would have killed her for having gone against what he had decided. Remember, too, the role of a woman back in the day we are talking, this makes what she did even more amazing.

Why did God intervene and strike Nabal? Even though the passage says that God struck Nabal ten days later, don't you think God had something to do with the original attack? Why did God intervene? I think that God knew that she had done what was right, he knew that Nabal would be livid about her intervening, and I think that God knew that great bodily harm, if not death were what awaited Abigail. God had to do something, there were no phones, she couldn't dial 9-1-1. None of Nabal's men were brave enough to go against Nabal.

I think that this story gives us great insight as to how God views the protection of abuse victims.

So, was Abigail an abuse victim? I would say that yes she was. You can tell that she feared his reactions, that is why she acted without consulting him. She may have had children, and we can tell that she went out of her way to protect the other men whom David planned to kill. If she truly despised her husband Nabal, she could have done nothing, hidden her kids (if she had some), waited it out and let David come and kill Nabal off and get rid of her problem. That would have made so much sense, however, there had to be some love and care – even for Nabal, because she chose to still do whatever she could to stop David and protect Nabal. I have made numerous arrests in domestic violence cases and the victim never wanted the abusive spouse arrested. There are many reasons why, many victims still love the abuser, have fun memories with the abuser, the victim just wants the abuse to end, and people on the outside looking in never quite understand or allow themselves to understand this dynamic in domestic violence.

Abusive relationship or troublesome marriage? You may be asking yourself, "Well, why did she marry such a jerk in the first place?" Good question, and one that we hear today as people try to intervene into domestic abuse situations. How do we know that she had any say in who she was marrying? It was very common, in those days, that a dowry would be paid for a wife and the woman had no say at all in whom she was marrying. Maybe he pretended to be nice while they were dating, and after the marriage his true colors shined through. Many abuse victims will tell you that their spouse never exhibited any signs of being abusive until after the marriage. Maybe she knew he was abusive but thought she could change him. Many victims have thought that perhaps they could tolerate the abuse that they first saw before marriage, and some really thought that the spouse would change or could be changed. Or, perhaps Nabal married Abigail, then moved her 500 miles away from her family and friends so that she would have no one to go to for advice and no support systems and no one who could just drop by and see that she had a bruise on her arm or a black eye. It is not uncommon for manipulating, controlling abusers to move quite a distance away from their spouse's friends and family to ensure total and complete dependence on the abuser and to make escape next to impossible.

Domestic abuse is rarely about today's event. When I train police officers to investigate domestic violence cases, we discuss not rushing the victim when asking them to recount what happened. Too many times we all want the victim to say what happened "just now" or "last night." When they stray and talk about past events, we oftentimes become like Joe Friday – "just the facts ma'am, only the facts."

The past is what helps us to understand what the victim is going through and gives us a better picture of the lethality of her situation. Oh, before we go any further, you will see me use the word she or her to refer to a victim, and you will read me using the term he or him as I discuss the abuser. The reason is that most victims ARE, in fact, women and MOST abusers are men. Can the woman be the abuser? YES, they can. Do we arrest women for domestic violence? The answer is yes. But by and large, in most cases, the abuser is the man. And, if you look at crime in general, who is responsible for most murders? Men. Who robs the most banks? Men. What gender is usually involved in a bar brawl? Men. So, please do not get too upset or hung up on the lack of gender neutrality in the text. Having said that, let's get back to past events. Today, the victim may have been yelled and screamed at, but yesterday she was pushed or punched, and last week she had a plate thrown at her and it missed her, but it broke into pieces all over the floor. So we use the past events to help us to understand what the victim is feeling right now.

Sharon couldn't believe it. It was 1:02 in the morning, she was still laying awake reading her book. She couldn't sleep tonight. Her husband Jeff was in bed next to her. He fell asleep before the news was even over. Then, an odd sound for this time of the morning – the phone. She jumped. Her heart raced a bit, "No one calls this late, I hope my mom is O.K." (Her mother had been hospitalized recently, and that was the first thing Sharon thought of.) But the phone call was much worse, much, much worse. There was an angry man on the phone who was demanding to talk to Jeff immediately. The man claimed to be the husband of Jeff's co-worker, and the man was insisting that he believed that his wife and Jeff were having an affair. Sharon could feel her heart racing, she had a deep pain in her stomach as she woke Jeff. Jeff was squinting and trying to understand what all was happening after just waking from a sound sleep. Sharon told him who was on the phone and Jeff quickly took the phone and went into the walk-in closet and partially shut the door. Sharon shook as she stood next to the door and listened in as Jeff angrily shouted into the phone. Jeff then cursed at the man and hung up the phone. Well, Sharon started asking Jeff what this was all about and if the allegation was true. Jeff snapped at her, and vehemently denied any affair and said that this guy was just paranoid. Sharon continued now to ask Jeff about the allegation and started to quiz him about times that he had left the house to "go to the store," but had returned with nothing. Jeff became very irate, jumped up out of bed and stormed downstairs and stood in the kitchen. He then sat down at the table and started to log onto his laptop computer. Sharon went to the kitchen, too. She was crying and just trying to reason with Jeff. She was saying that how could she not be upset and wondering what was going on with this strange call in the middle of the night.

Let's stop here. So far, has Jeff done anything that he could be arrested for? The answer so far is no. He has broken no law, he may or may not be guilty of cheating on his wife – so far, that was just an allegation and we do not know how that husband arrived at that conclusion. We can say that there may be some strong, compelling evidence for the guy to think something has happened, after all he called Jeff at one in the morning to confront him. But I think we can all agree that Jeff has not committed a crime so far.

But, Sharon quizzes him some more. She isn't even shouting, she is calm so far, but still troubled by the whole situation. Suddenly, Jeff has had quite enough. He slams the lid of his laptop down, he stands up, slams his open hand down on the table, gets within inches of Sharon's face and screams for her to shut up, and he starts screaming and swearing at her. He moves closer to her as she backs away. Now he starts chasing her around the kitchen table, swearing and screaming at her. She dashes to the right, Jeff moves towards her, and she stops and goes to the left. He is now moving towards her the other way. OK, let's stop here. Has Jeff broken any laws now? The answer is yes. You may be asking yourself how. Is this abuse? Just a troublesome marriage? If this same situation were occurring at work with a co-worker instead of at home with his wife, what would happen to Jeff? Would someone call the police and say that there was a disturbance taking place? Would Jeff likely get a ticket for disorderly conduct and possibly face suspension or termination from work? The answer to these questions is yes. What if this same event were playing out at the restaurant? Let's say you are with your family, the waitress has just brought you your food, and at the corner table of the diner there's a guy screaming and swearing at a woman whom he is chasing around the table. Are you concerned? Are you trying to keep your kids from seeing and hearing this? Are you or any other patrons dialing 9-1-1 on their cell phones, or demanding the manager call the police? I think we can all agree that the answers to these questions are also yes.

Are you or any other patrons approaching the pair and trying to get them to calm down? You may say yes but you are in the minority. Most people do not want to get involved, or they fear that the aggressor here may turn on them. Let's face it, here is an angry, aggressive person and there are plenty of knives and forks laying around.

Now, back to Sharon and Jeff's house. Jeff is still screaming, swearing, and chasing his wife around the kitchen table. Sharon is afraid that their kids will wake up and come downstairs and witness this. She is afraid for her safety and sees the kitchen phone handset on the counter and decides to give up the safety of being on the other side of the table and grab the phone. She could call her sister or Jeff's mom or, need be, she could dial 9-1-1. She runs for the counter, grabs the phone, Jeff follows, charges at her, grabs her upper arm and then glares at her. Sharon has seen this glare before, and now she is really scared. You see, Jeff grabbed her arm and glared at Sharon like that three years ago in August when he grabbed her throat and strangled her. He cut off her oxygen back then for several seconds. She thought sure that she would die. She never called the police, she never told anyone, except for her sister, whom she confided in almost a year later. She even took a photo of a red mark on her neck right after it happened, and she still has the photo hidden in her jewelry box. Sharon feels like this is it, Jeff is going to strangle her tonight and she fears that she will die. Sharon dials 9-1-1, the call goes through, but the dispatcher only hears yelling and screaming in the background and then the line goes dead. The 9-1-1 computer system, though, shows on the screen the address where the call originated and police are sent to check the home for a "9-1-1 hang-up, unknown disturbance."

Officers arrive to find the attached garage door going up and a male holding a computer laptop and opening a car door. One officer meets Jeff in the garage while the other officer meets Sharon at the front door. Sharon is visibly shaken and explains everything that has happened. Jeff, on the other hand, is calm, collected, saying that his wife is crazy and saying that nothing happened. The officers meet for a moment to share information gathered so far and the decision is made to arrest Jeff for Domestic Violence related - Disorderly Conduct and Intimidation of a Victim.

When the officers tell Jeff that he is under arrest, he changes from being nice to yelling and swearing at them. He is handcuffed and placed into the back of the squad car. He demands to know the charges and officers explained – Disorderly Conduct and Intimidation of a Victim. He wants to know what he did wrong. The officer explains that his actions, yelling and swearing at her, chasing her around the table, constituted fear in her and a disorderly situation. Jeff, like most abusers, then gets angrier and asks the officer, "Oh, and I suppose you never have a disagreement with your wife or anyone else?" (In just about every case that I have dealt with, the abuser has asked a question like this of the arresting officer. The abuser wants the officer to answer the question in the affirmative, in order to bring validity to what the abuser has done. And the simple answer is that "yes," we all have disagreements, but a majority of conflicts do not and should not become loud, profane disturbances.)

Jeff pushes the officer more and asks why he is being arrested for Domestic Violence. The officer tells him that his wife felt afraid of the situation and felt more afraid because she had once been strangled by him in the past. Jeff pounds his head against the squad cage a couple of times and screams, "You arrested me for a feeling???!!! I'm going to jail because of a feeling???!!!"

And that is, indeed, by law in most states what starts the process of making the charge of Domestic Abuse. How the victim feels in terms of danger and fear is an element that helps determine the law enforcement response.

But there is more to this story than the strangulation in the past and the chase around the kitchen table. After the one officer leaves with Jeff to take him to jail, Sharon explains to the officer that they have been married for six years. She said that after they were married Jeff changed. He became very controlling, telling her how long she could talk on the phone. He refused to allow her to work, and all decisions, even where they would go to dinner or what T.V. show they would watch, was completely dictated by Jeff. She said that she has lived six years with her mouth shut, because anytime she has ever said anything or tried to share her opinion, Jeff becomes angry and storms around the house giving her the silent treatment. Sharon said, "I've spent my married life walking on egg shells, just trying to survive one more day, one more contact with my own husband."

So, now that you know that, let's pretend that the chase around the kitchen table and the strangulation incident had never happened. Is Jeff an abuser? Just a participant in a troubled marriage? A candidate for marital counseling? Would he even go to marital counseling? Most abusive people like this flat out refuse to go. Do you know why? Because they like the way things are going now. And why not, everything is all about them. They get to decide everything, control everything, they totally get their way in all things. And if a wife like Sharon is never slapped, punched or killed, what is her quality of life? What impact on her emotional state and physical state is this environment having on her?

Let me introduce you to Sally. She is staring at her watch, waiting for a green light. She is sweating, she feels tense, her stomach is churning. Just a couple more miles she tells herself. "Finally, I swear that's the longest red light in town," Sally tells herself as she proceeds through the intersection. Sally pulls into the driveway, she gathers her things, she gets to the side door, she pauses a minute, "Please don't be mad, please don't be mad," she whispers to herself as she is about to turn the door knob. She takes a huge, deep breath, exhales, another deep breath, and an exhale, she opens the door, and there he is, Roger, sitting at the kitchen table. He is looking at the clock, he is tapping his fingers on the table. Sally feels her heart race, she has a sharp pain in her stomach, "Oh, my ulcer again," she says to herself.

Roger rolls his eyes, sighs deeply and asks, "Do you know what time it is?"

Sally blurts out, "I know, it's 5:40, I'm late, I'm so sorry."

Roger reminds her, "You know, when you took this job, it was against my better judgment, and I told you that this was gonna happen."

Sally puts her purse down on the table and says, "I really tried to leave on time, but my boss needed me to change her PowerPoint presentation, and I'm the only one who knows how to."

Roger rolls his eyes and asks, "And how is that my problem? I'm hungry, the kids are starved, they still haven't done their homework, you can't put one more dish in either sink, the clothes hamper is heaping over, and I have dart league tonight."

Sally tries to diffuse the situation, she says, "Of course, you are right, let me whip up something real quick for us to eat, and then I'll start picking up around here, I'm just so sorry."

"Well, this isn't the first time. For a part-time job, you sure end up working a lot, and you need to tell your boss that you need to leave on time, and if you can't do that, I'll be happy to call her for you, otherwise, if this kind of thing is gonna happen all the time, well, you are just gonna have to quit!" Roger stands up after saying this and says, "No, don't try to cook anything, it will take too long and even the counter tops are too cluttered. Order out something."

Sally says, "O.K., how about Chinese?"

Roger scowls and says, "I hate Chinese." (News to Sally, he always seemed to like it.) Roger says, "Order a pizza, how long do you think it will take you to order it and pick it up?"

Sally grabs the phone book and replies, "Well, if I call now, it shouldn't take long at all."

Roger opens his wallet, hands her a twenty and says, "Here, I'll pay for it, you call it in, leave, and we should see you back here in 25 minutes." He walks away, rolling his eyes, then says, "I'm really thinking that you working isn't the best thing for us and I'm going to be re-evaluating this whole situation."

Sally makes the call, she knows that there is no way a pizza can be made, picked up and her back here with it in 25 minutes, but she just can't approach Roger, so off she races, tears in her eyes, knowing that she is going to fail in this, too.

O.K., now, did Roger do anything that he can be arrested for? No, he hasn't, he didn't physically harm Sally, he has broken no laws.

Can or should Roger really think that he can determine and decide whether or not Sally should work? I would say no. He likes the extra money, but what he really wants is someone to have dinner ready for him when he gets home. What he really wants is for Sally to spend her day cleaning and taking care of the kids.

Let's talk about Roger. Why didn't he cook something or order out? Why didn't he load the dishwasher and do some laundry? Well, Roger thinks that these tasks are below him, that these are Sally's jobs. Would the whole thing work better if Roger just helped out and accepted the fact that once in a while Sally may be late? Why doesn't Roger do this? The answer is that he is a controller, he likes to call the shots.

What about Sally? She loves her children, she loves Roger, but at the same time she hates how she is treated. She has no say in many of the day-to-day operations of home life. But at work she is so valued, people compliment her on how well she does her job. She walks into work and feels so esteemed that she just has never felt that at home with Roger. Now, the one thing that brings her so much reward and joy she may lose as she just heard Roger say that HE was going to "re-evaluate" whether she should work or not. So she tells herself that she just won't be late anymore, but she knows that it is not reasonable to believe that that will happen because, from time to time, emergencies come up and her boss relies on her.

So, is Sally abused? Just in a troubled marriage? What if I told you that Roger usually goes out to her car everyday and checks her odometer reading? That's right, he checks her mileage each day, quizzes her as to where she had been and even MapQuests her destinations to see if it all matches up.

What if I told you that when Sally is home, when Roger walks in the door, he immediately picks up the phone and dials *69 to see who the last person to call the house was, and he then hits "redial" and checks to see whom Sally last talked to. He checks her cell phone history, he listens to her voice mail. One time when they were driving somewhere together, she was in the passenger seat and at a red light she glanced over at the car stopped at their right. Roger slammed his hand on the steering wheel and angrily yelled, "What, do you want to sleep with that guy? Why are you looking at him??!!"

Roger is a controller and Sally is a victim of verbal and mental abuse. I mentioned earlier that an abusive incident is rarely about the situation right now; the history of the relationship and the pattern of events is what really matters. These examples help show you what I am talking about and should be understood when talking to victims of domestic violence.

I ran into a woman that I know last week. I have been friends of her and her husband for about 14 years. I know that David can be harsh with people, I've even seen him blow up at Carol. I asked her how they were doing and she said, "Well, Dave's health isn't the greatest, and he's still a real pistol to live with. I walk around the house like I'm walking on egg shells. I'm too old to do anything about it now, but our entire 31 years of marriage have just been an awful nightmare."

How sad I thought. I saw her lip quiver as she told me that. A tear formed in the corner of her eye. As far as I know, there has never been any physical violence, but just talking to her, you see a badly beat up woman, a woman who never dreamed that her life would be so sad.

And where does that "walking on egg shells" thing come from? One night about a year ago I personally responded to three different homes for domestic disturbances. Would you believe that each victim said of the events that led up to the violence, "I was walking on egg shells."

Abuse victims say that this feeling is one of just trying to survive, that if they say anything the abuser will snap; if they say nothing the abuser will snap. They cower around, just trying to survive, just trying to keep their kids safe.

But do any of these feelings constitute the commission of any crime? And the answer is no. If you suggested to any of these victims that they need to ask their spouse to join them for marriage counseling, would the abuser go? In my 22 years of experience dealing with abusers the answer is no. The reasons are simple for the abuser. First of all, they do not see what they are doing as abuse and, secondly, they like how things are going. They like having THEIR way ALL of the time and they know that counseling may lead to some compromising on their part and they see this as a threat to their way of life.

So, where does that leave the victim? How will anything ever change in their life? Are they really just stuck because they said, "I do?" And, even if they are never physically killed by their abuser, haven't they already been killed mentally and emotionally and are they not suffering through a long, painful and torturous death?

The next chapter will explain by legal definition what Domestic Abuse is.

Chapter Two

What Is Domestic Abuse?

IT WAS A HOT JULY evening in 1987. I was patrolling through a subdivision, I had my driver's side window down, there were families out in their yards playing. It was still light out, but I could see kids with mason jars, standing in their yards, just waiting to catch the first firefly of the evening. It seemed like the perfect night.

Well, almost perfect. As I rounded a curve and came up the next street, I heard a loud crashing sound like breaking glass. I glanced to my left and the brown brick ranch with the green shutters looked a little odd as a brass lamp complete with a light beige shade came flying out of the front livingroom picture window. Loud screams of an angry man and the wails and sobs of a crying woman were bellowing from the inside of the house.

I quickly radioed for backup. I gave my location and parked a few houses up the road. I approached the house. The yelling was still very loud and very profane. Other neighbors out watering their tomato plants were now standing in their driveways, swatting mosquitoes and trying to get a glimpse of what was happening. I recognized this house. We had been here before. Just about every officer on every shift had been here before. This was the home of Richard and Carol, neighbors were used to the fights, and this was going to turn out, I was sure, just like the last time. She would have an injury of some sort, Richard would be drunk and swearing at us, with an "I'm untouchable" assurance. We will ask Carol if she wants to go to the hospital, she will say no. We will ask her if she wants to press charges, she will say no. We will leave with Richard in the garage, smoking a cigar and downing another beer laughing at us, because he will have won again.

And I was right. Her glasses were broken, she had a bruise on the outside of her left eye. Her right forearm was bleeding because Richard had thrown her down to the floor in the kitchen. We stood above her as she was trying to pick up shards of glass from the wooden floor in the living room next to the front window and she kept saying, "Just please leave, I'll be alright."

We reminded her of the local battered women's shelter, and she again said, "No, thank you, I'll be O.K."

This was a scenario that played itself out all over the State of Wisconsin, every day and every night until 1989 when mandatory arrest laws were adopted by the State Legislature, thus changing how law enforcement could respond to domestic violence calls.

Other states in this country had already adopted these laws and all states now have them, thanks to victim advocacy groups/agencies, prosecutors, law enforcement and the Violence Against Women Act. There are countless other people, including elected representatives, who funded programs, and if I have left anyone or any group out, I apologize.

Again, I can only speak for the laws in Wisconsin, but they are quite similar across the country. And in those early days of the new law, in the county where I work, when we received a call for a domestic violence incident there was a mandatory arrest if we had probable cause to believe that a crime was committed and fit into the confines of Domestic Violence. It was new territory for many counties, and in the first few years after we figured out who the victim was and arrested the perpetrator, we had to take the offender to jail. He/she had to be fingerprinted and photographed. We had to offer the victim a 24 hour no contact form. If the victim signed the form asking that there be no contact, the offender, even if able to bond out of jail, was temporarily restrained from having ANY contact with the victim. The offender received a citation, through our local municipal court, for $625.00. Once the bond was paid, the offender could leave jail. If they could not pay the bond that night, the offender would have to see the municipal judge the next day to get a signature bond.

This system was flawed in many ways because the municipal judge could not place an offender on probation. If an offender showed up in court with the victim and said, "Gee, we worked things out," the court would greatly reduce the fine or dismiss it altogether. There was a local doctor who provided an anger management type class, and if the offender agreed to pay for the class in lieu of the fine, the case would be dismissed that way. But if the offender only went to one or two classes and never went back, there were no teeth in the procedure to make sure that they attended the full course.

Another issue with the citation for $625.00 was that many of these domestic fights started because of financial problems and the fine just caused greater financial hardship on the families of those involved. I had even heard from victims who were no longer calling, that the abuse had not stopped, but they had quit calling because of the large fine and that nothing had really changed as a result of our intervention.

In our county, several years later, the District Attorney ordered that there be no more tickets issued and that all domestic violence related charges be sent to their office. The State of Wisconsin had also changed the temporary No Contact Provision to a 72 hour instead of the old 24 hour time frame. This allowed more time for a victim to apply for a long-term restraining order, and once it was drafted and served, it could be done in three days which means that there is the potential that an abuser can be kept away from the victim quicker and longer.

The same couple that I just described, I remember going to their house on another domestic disturbance after the new law. The neighbor had called in loud screaming and yelling. When we arrived, the wife had a slap mark across her face. The husband stood there with his usual smirk and he apparently had not heard about the new law. When he realized we were handcuffing him and telling him that he was going to jail, he flipped out and was screaming at his wife, "Why did you press charges on me?" We told him that it wasn't her, it was US, that the State of Wisconsin was the one pressing charges. He was quite angry and, for him, it was because no one had ever held him accountable for his behavior before. When he was a boy, I'm sure someone at home or school told him that boys don't hit girls and now, finally, someone was calling him on his behavior. I still recall that his wife, after seeing him escorted out of the house, said that every time we had been there before she wanted to say something, she wanted to do something. She knew that what was happening to her was wrong, but that had she said anything she felt that her husband would kill her once he got out of jail.

So, Domestic Abuse, mandatory arrest happens when the following criteria is met:

- Did a crime occur? Does the officer have probable cause to believe that a crime was committed? Probable Cause is not Beyond a Reasonable Doubt which is necessary for a jury to find someone guilty. Probable Cause is simply defined as, have you as a police officer seen and heard enough to believe, as a reasonable officer or person, that something happened here which violated any laws?

- Is the relationship domestic? Are the two married? Have they ever been married? Are they two adults living together? Are they two adults who maintain separate apartments or houses, but spend the night from time to time with one another? Do they not live together but have a child in common? All of these questions are asked by the officers and if the answer to any of them is "yes," then it is a domestic relationship. Even if two adults are in college together, they are both 19 and share a dorm room, they are adults residing together and the reason that it is domestic is because, if the officers do not arrest one, the victim is still stuck in a potentially violent atmosphere. If an arrest is made, once the offender is out of jail, the offender may want to retaliate against the victim and the victim is stuck there because of housing arrangements.

In Wisconsin, if the offender is 17 years old and the victim is an adult, the 17 year old is treated as an adult, charged and taken to jail. I can think of several instances over the years when a 15 year old son comes in after curfew, his mom confronts him on it and he punches his mom in the mouth. We arrive and mom doesn't want anything done, just for the police to tell him to go to his room. He continues to hit his mom, and when he is 16, the police get called there again after he pushes his mom to the floor. Again, the police can do nothing if the mom does not want to pursue anything. But Johnny gets a wake-up call when he is 17 now and he punches his mom. He always thought he could get away with it, and mom still doesn't want him arrested, but police have no choice. And, hopefully, it sends an early message to this teen abuser that domestic violence is not acceptable and hopefully his future wife has been spared some abuse.

But, if the victim is 17 and the abuser is an adult, the 17 year old is treated as a child and the abuser is arrested for Child Abuse, which is another crime which does not need the victim to press charges, the State is the complainant.

- Does the officer reasonably believe there is a likelihood of continued abuse (bodily harm, sexual assault, impairment or threat of harm or assault) against the victim? There are hardly any heated, abusive situations that would not lead anyone to believe that there is a threat of continued violence. These are not simple disagreements, these are scary situations where someone is being physically beaten, threatened, or a hole has been punched into the wall. When law enforcement arrives on a scene, the offenders tend to calm down and be on their best behavior, but in reality, if the officers were to just leave and do nothing, there is no doubt, in a majority of cases, that the situation will continue and likely escalate.

- Is there evidence of physical injury to the victim? If officers receive a 9-1-1 call because neighbors hear loud screaming and crying coming from the apartment next door, and once the officers arrive, they see a shaken, crying woman standing in the kitchen with a ripped shirt and a scratch or bruise on her arm and she and her husband say, "Nothing is happening, we do not even know why someone would have called," there is enough for the officer to reasonably believe that something happened there and that there is a likelihood of continued abuse if they leave and do nothing.

- Was the crime committed in the past 28 days? I'm not sure what the mandatory Arrest time frame is in other states, but the legislature in Wisconsin picked 28 days. These are not the same as Statutes of Limitations. The Statutes of Limitations are three years for a misdemeanor charge and six years for charges that would be a felony. So, let's say a women disclosed to a law enforcement officer that 4 years ago her husband broke her leg. She continues that she did go to the emergency room and was in a cast, but she told the nurses and the doctor that she had fallen on ice. That could be charged out as a felony substantial battery, and because it falls within six years of the commission of the crime, the abuser can be arrested. That doesn't mean necessarily that a jury would convict because the defense is going to be that she is lying. But the jury may convict and, who knows, she may have written the account down in a journal at the time, or she may have told a co-worker or relative whom she had sworn to secrecy, and they could be called as witnesses.

The 28 day Mandatory Arrest usually comes about in the following way: Deputies respond to a domestic disturbance call and arrest the offender for battery because the victim discloses that she was just punched in the face. But while the officers are talking to her, they see what appears to be a week old or so bruise on her arm and another on her leg. When they ask her about these old injuries, she says that one week ago there was another argument and he kicked her leg, and three days before that he squeezed her arm. Each of these previously un-reported incidents can be charged out and a Mandatory Arrest made now on all three, because all three occurred within 28 days.

So the magic part of the 28 days is that a Mandatory Arrest can be made, and it does not require the victim to sign a complaint – the State is the complainant.

Any violation of a restraining order or a temporary restraining order are also Mandatory Arrests. We'll discuss restraining orders more in another chapter.

The laws then that Law Enforcement can consider at the scene are as follows:

Disorderly Conduct - Wisconsin Statute 947.01

"Whoever, in a public or private place, engages in violent, abusive, indecent, profane, boisterous, unreasonably loud or otherwise disorderly conduct under circumstances in which the conduct tends to cause or provoke a disturbance is guilty of a Class B Misdemeanor."

Everyone has a disagreement, but in healthy conflicts no one is throwing things around the room, screaming at the top of their lungs and calling their spouse vulgar and obscene names. And this particular statute is hard for many to comprehend. The church community will often tell the victim of this kind of abuse that they are simply stuck in a difficult marriage. The abusers will oftentimes participate in conduct, which intentionally falls short of punching or pushing their spouse, because they know that they can be arrested for battery, and they try to believe that they are not abusers so long as they fall short of going physical. The interesting thing is that when I have arrested someone for Domestic Violence related Disorderly Conduct, they yell and scream in the back seat of the squad car, while on the way to jail that, "It's my house, I can say anything and do anything I want to in MY house!!!" I will then confront them on that statement and ask them this question: If this same incident and loud, profane activity occurred at work, towards a co-worker or boss, what would happen? Each time, the arrested person will look down and say, "Well, if this same thing happened at work I'd get fired." And I will ask, what would happen if the same argument, at the same intensity, occurred in the corner grocery store or at a restaurant? The abuser will usually say, "Well, people would probably tell the manager, run out or call 9-1-1 on their cell phones." I will then say that they now understood what disorderly conduct is and that the law's very provisions are for a public place or a private place.

As Disorderly Conduct like this relates over to church, I have had abusers who proclaim to be "good church members" or even a "church deacon" say that what happens in their house is their business. All arguing stops, though, when I say, "Gee, the Bible says that we as married couples are one flesh with one another, so to you it's O.K. to treat people at work and in the public better than you should treat someone who is one flesh with you?"

The bond amount in Wisconsin on this charge if $150.00. The arrested person must be fingerprinted and photographed and must post the bond, in cash, before being released.

Disorderly Conduct is usually any activity that prompts someone in the home to call the police or a neighbor to call the police. Again, to those who would say that couples cannot even have a disagreement anymore, I would say there has to be a lot of overt, scary things going on to make someone pick up the phone and dial 9-1-1.

Damage to Property – 943.01

(1) Whoever intentionally causes damage to any physical property of another without the person's consent is guilty of a Class A Misdemeanor." (If the property adds up to damage of $2,500.00 or more, it is a felony charge.)

Bill and Marcy are having a discussion, the discussion turns to a heated argument and Bill gets so mad that he decides to punch a hole in the wall. Or, Bill takes a vase off of the table and launches it across the room and it breaks into pieces. Bill can be charged with Disorderly Conduct because of the abusive, profane argument that led up to the damage and he can be charged with Damage to Property.

When I have arrested someone for such damage, 99.9 percent of the time the abuser will yell at me and say, "It's my house, and if I want to punch a hole in every wall, I can and I will!!" But the truth is, according to the law, he is damaging "community property" which means "property of another – which is property in which a person other than the actor has a legal interest in which the actor has no right to defeat or impair, **even though the actor may also have a legal interest in the property.**" (Section 939.22(28) WI Stats.)

I've even arrested a person for damage to property and the suspect will say that the T.V. he broke was his before marriage, and that it is HIS property. But under marital property, everything acquired after marriage or brought together through marriage is now property of each person.

And if the property damaged was an expensive 52" plasma television worth $2,500.00, the damage is a felony count.

So, Bill would be taken to jail, booked and charged with Damage to Property, and the bond to get out would be $300.00. And if the damage amount made it a felony, then there would be no bond and he would have to sit in jail overnight and see a court commissioner the next day. The court commissioner can impose that bond to be paid for release, or he/she could release Bill on a signature bond.

If Bill was drinking, the court commissioner would likely impose a bond condition of "no drinking" and/or "no taverns," and in a felony case, the court would usually impose a no contact order with the victim, which means that Bill could not go home until the court changes the order.

Here is where we see offender accountability. When an arrest is made, law enforcement is telling him that what he did was wrong. When a court commissioner or judge tells the offender that what they did was wrong, and that they now have restrictions placed on them, the offender who really wants to change will finally see that they need to change something.

The no-contact order with the victim gives safety from the offender and empowers the victim to look at options that she may have. How many times have you wondered why an abused person would stay with an abuser? We are going to go into depth on that in another chapter, but oftentimes it is because the victim knows that the offender will be released from jail, back at home, and even more angry because an arrest was made.

Battery; substantial battery; aggravated battery – 940.19

(1) Whoever causes bodily harm to another by an act done with intent to cause bodily harm to another without the consent of the person so harmed is guilty of a Class A Misdemeanor. The injury can be visible such as a cut, scratch or start of a bruise, but some abusers pull hair in attempt to not leave a mark. A simple feeling of pain will suffice as injury.

(2) Whoever causes substantial bodily harm to another by an act done with intent to cause bodily harm to that person or another is guilty of a class I Felony. A chipped tooth, a wound requiring sutures, a fractured bone, bruise, contusion.

(4) Great bodily harm statute which is a Class H Felony. Injuries requiring surgery, or multiple sutures. Strangulation of a victim would also apply, but in some strangulations, the case could be more severe and could be a **Class E Felony.**

OR – (6) Whoever intentionally causes <u>bodily</u> (notice, not great bodily, just bodily) harm to another by conduct that creates a substantial <u>risk</u> of great bodily harm is guilty of a Class H Felony. A rebuttable presumption of conduct creating a substantial risk of great bodily harm arises:

(a) If the person harmed is 62 years of age or older; or

(b) If the person harmed has a physical disability, whether congenital or acquired by accident, injury or disease, that is discernible by an ordinary person viewing the physically disabled person, or that is actually known by the actor.

So, you can see that the legislature thought it important to put into place special protections for older victims and disabled victims.

But what about pregnant women? Did you know that many first-time pregnant women are abused physically by their partners? Some abusers who are very controlling resent the attention that they see will be diverted away from them, and instead given to the new baby.

There is in Wisconsin:

Battery to an unborn child; substantial battery to an unborn child;

Aggravated battery to an unborn child – 940.195

(1) Whoever causes bodily harm to an unborn child by an act done with intent to cause bodily harm to that unborn child, to the woman who is pregnant with that unborn child or another is guilty of a Class A Misdemeanor.

There are three more subsections which make it a felony charge to cause great bodily harm, and subsection six reads:

(6) Whoever intentionally causes bodily harm to an unborn child by conduct that creates a substantial risk of great bodily harm is guilty of a Class H Felony.

So, let's say that an abuser kicks at his pregnant wife's stomach, she anticipates where the kick might land and she moves to protect the unborn baby, but a slight injury occurred to the baby because he still slightly hit the unborn baby. This subsection says that this is a felony because the actor knew that there was **a substantial risk of great bodily harm.**

Sexual Assault – 940.225

There are some people who say that a wife cannot be sexually assaulted by her husband. I can tell you that I have dealt with many marital rape cases, and there are countless victims out there who have never said anything to anyone.

Holly is home alone, again, on another Friday night. Her husband, Anthony, gets done with work at 4:30 in the evening and goes out to bars with his co-workers. Holly put the kids to bed, washed the dishes and did a few loads of laundry. She watched T.V. for a while and didn't dare call Anthony. She knows that he shuts his cell phone off when he is out with friends, and in the past when she has tried to reach him he has become furious, and when he did come home he screamed and yelled at her and twisted her arm.

Holly goes to bed at about 3:00 a.m. Just like every other Friday night, Anthony staggers in the door, gets into bed, doesn't speak a word, and the next thing she knows he is on top of her, now he is pulling up her nightgown and then he is inside of her. She is in great pain, just like other times, but tonight she pushes him off and says "no," but Anthony ignores her and refuses to stop. Holly was raped, and on the other nights, too, and this falls under:

940.225 (3) Third Degree Sexual Assault. Whoever has sexual intercourse with a person without the consent of that person is guilty of a Class G Felony.

The class of felony increases if there is use of a weapon or threat of use of a weapon. And sub six reads:

(6) MARRIAGE NOT A BAR TO PROSECUTION. A defendant shall not be presumed to be incapable of violating this section because of marriage to the complainant.

I have had many discussions with elders and even some pastors as sometimes the position of the church is that "she cannot deprive sex or her body from her husband." Church leaders and even abusers who attend church will often throw out the Apostle Paul's words from 1Corinthians 7:5 which reads: "Do not deprive each other except by mutual consent and for a time, so that you may devote yourselves to prayer." Anthony was not devoting himself to prayer while he was away from Holly, he was out devoting himself to himself, hanging out and drinking with his friends while Holly was stuck at home. There was no romance in that encounter and it was forced upon her.

Mayhem – 940.21

Whoever, with intent to disable or disfigure another, cuts or mutilates the tongue, ear, nose, lip, limb or other bodily member of another is guilty of a Class C Felony.

We usually see Mayhem when an offender breaks a beer bottle and cuts the victim's face, or puts out a cigarette butt onto the victim's skin, or bites the victim's face leaving bite marks. I've had abusers say, "Why are you holding me on a felony charge, yes, I burned her with my cigarette butt, but isn't that just disorderly conduct?" You see, even some abusers think that they know what they may be able to get away with if the police happen to get called.

Reckless Injury – 940.23

(1) FIRST – DEGREE RECKLESS INJURY,

(1) Whoever recklessly causes great bodily harm to another human being under circumstances which show utter disregard for human life is guilty of a Class D Felony.

(b) Whoever recklessly causes great bodily harm to an unborn child under circumstances that show utter disregard for the life of that unborn child, the woman who is pregnant with that unborn child or another is guilty of a Class D Felony.

So, if the abuser is driving with the victim as a passenger, and the abuser is arguing and driving crazy, going into ditches or almost hitting trees or oncoming cars in an attempt to scare the victim and an accident occurs, leading to great bodily harm to the victim, the abuser was aware that his conduct was imminently dangerous to another's safety or life, even if he did not intend the actual consequences.

Injury by Negligent Handling of Dangerous Weapon, Explosives or Fire – 940.24

(1) Whoever causes bodily harm to another by the negligent operation or handling of a dangerous weapon, explosive or fire is guilty of a Class I Felony.

(2) Whoever causes bodily harm to an unborn child by the negligent operation or handling of a dangerous weapon, explosives or fire is guilty of a Class I Felony.

I had a case where the abuser had the victim trapped in the corner of a room. He didn't like her new hair color, and he actually set her hair on fire with a cigarette lighter. And this felony charge does not require GREAT bodily harm, just bodily harm.

And while we are talking about fire, there is:

Arson of property other than building – 943.03

Whoever, by means of fire, intentionally damages any property of another without the person's consent, if the property is not a building and has a value of $100 or more, is guilty of a Class I Felony.

It is 3:45 p.m. and Krissy is at work. She received a frantic phone call from her 14 year old daughter, Taylor, who is at home. Her daughter is screaming, saying, "MOM, MOM! you have to do something, dad went nuts, he's out in the back yard at the fire pit and he is burning all of your stuff!!" Sure enough, Danny is out in the back yard with a huge burn pile and he is throwing in Krissy's dresses, her underwear, her make-up kit and bed sheets. Krissy can't believe it, but deep down inside she thought that something would happen. She had just hung up on him about 15 minutes before. Danny was mad at her about something and had called her at work, 20 times in a half hour, yelling and swearing at her. Krissy hung up as she knew that the conversation was going nowhere, and her boss was now giving her a glare as he knew how much time she was spending away from her work. Krissy calls 9-1-1 and asks the police to intervene. When officers arrive, Danny is dragging the kitchen island out of the dining room sliding glass doors. He is arrested for a felony Arson count.

False Imprisonment – 940.30

Whoever intentionally confines or restrains another without the person's consent and with knowledge that he has no lawful authority to do so is guilty of a Class H Felony.

Ralph and Jan are driving home and Ralph, while driving, is pounding his fist on the steering wheel and reaching over with his right hand to hit Jan who is in the passenger seat. Jan is terrified and every time that Ralph stops for a stop sign or red light, Jan opens the car door to try to get out and call the police. When she opens the door, Ralph speeds up to keep her in the car. There is not only a battery and disorderly conduct charge, but a False Imprisonment charge because he is confining her and keeping her from freedom of movement.

Alex and Terri just had a heated argument and Alex slapped her. Terri is afraid of him and tries to get to the phone to call 9-1-1. Alex quickly grabs her arms and holds her against her will for several minutes in an attempt to keep her from leaving the house or calling anyone. This is False Imprisonment.

Taking Hostages – 940.305

(1) Whoever by force or threat of imminent force seizes, confines, or restrains a person without the person's consent and with the intent to use the person as a hostage in order to influence a person to perform or not to perform some action demanded by the actor is guilty of a Class B Felony.

Mike has abused his wife and two children for several years, and his wife Laura just got the courage to move out. She brought her kids to her parents' house and she then went to work. Mike came home and found Laura's note that told him that she had left. Mike is furious and went to Laura's work, waited for her to come out, and when she was in the parking lot he pulled up next to her, pulled her into his car and demanded to know where the kids were. When she told him that they were at her parents' house, he drove there, parked in front of their house and called his mother-in-law on his cell phone. He told Laura's mom that he had her daughter in the car and he would release Laura only if she brought their kids out to the car.

Kidnapping – 940.31

(1) Whoever by use of force or threat of force carries another from one place to another without his or her consent and with intent to cause him or her to be secretly confined or imprisoned or to be carried out of this state or to be held to service against his or her will is guilty of a Class B Felony.

In a domestic violence case, if the victim were sexually abused and transported over the border to Illinois or Minnesota, for example, this charge could apply. Since the courts have ruled that sexual assault constitutes "service against will," a defendant who sexually assaults a victim in a home after preventing her from leaving may be charged with kidnapping. If a defendant harms the victim in an automobile, demands that she accompany him or drive him to another state, and won't let the victim out of the car, the actor can be charged with kidnapping.

Intimidation of Witness – 940.42 and 940.43

Whoever knowingly and maliciously prevents or dissuades, or who attempts to so prevent or dissuade any witness from attending or giving testimony at any trial, proceeding or inquiry authorized by law is guilty of a Class A Misdemeanor.

There is a Felony provision in 940.43 if the actor's act is accompanied by force or violence, or attempted force or violence, upon the witness or the spouse, child, stepchild, foster child, treatment foster child, parent, sibling or grandchild of the witness or any person sharing a common domicile with the witness. There is also a provision for the actor using injury or damage to the real or personal property of another person.

Doug is hitting his wife, and their 10 year old daughter wakes up and hears her mom crying for help. Their daughter dials 9-1-1, the police are responding and she goes downstairs and tells her parents to quit fighting and says that the police are coming. Doug is arrested, and after his release from jail, grabs his daughter and tells her that if she testifies in court, about what she saw and heard here, that she is going to say that nothing happened, that she made it all up.

Intimidation of Victim – 940.44

Whoever knowingly and maliciously prevents or dissuades, or who attempts to so prevent or dissuade, another person who has been the victim of any crime or who is acting on behalf of the victim from doing any of the following is guilty of a Class A Misdemeanor:

(1) Making any report of the victimization to any peace officer or state, local or federal law enforcement or prosecuting agency or judge.

(2) Causing a complaint, indictment or information to be sought and prosecuted and assisting in the prosecution thereof.

(3) Arresting or causing or seeking the arrest of any person in connection with the victimization.

Paul grabs his wife's throat and she was able to grab the phone and dial 9-1-1. The call went through to the sheriff dispatcher, but Paul hung up the phone before she could say anything. The officers are on their way to a "9-1-1 hang-up, problem unknown" call. The fact that Paul disconnected the call is Intimidation of a Victim.

There is a felony provision under **940.45** if the actor breaks the phone to prevent the victim from making the call. And in such a case there would also be the Damage to Property charge since the phone was jointly owned by the husband and wife.

Endangering Safety by Use of Dangerous Weapon – 941.20

(1) Whoever does any of the following is guilty of a Class A Misdemeanor:

(a) Endangers another's safety by the negligent operation or handling of a dangerous weapon; or

(b) Operates or goes armed with a firearm while he or she is under the influence of an intoxicant; or

(c) Intentionally points a firearm at or toward another.

There is a Felony provision under **(2)**: if the actor: **Intentionally discharges a firearm into a vehicle or building under circumstances in which he or she should realize there might be a human being present therein; or sets a spring gun.**

There are many cases where an upset abuser pulls out a gun, and the gun does not have to be loaded or even capable of firing. It is the fear and intimidation that a firearm has that is the important part of this statute.

Carrying Concealed Weapon – 941.23

Any person except a peace officer who goes armed with a concealed and dangerous weapon is guilty of a Class A Misdemeanor.

This would not apply to the states that have conceal-carry laws which allow a licensed permit holder to carry a concealed weapon, but if the actor is not in such a state, or in a state that allows it, but he/she has no permit, it is a violation. So if a victim tells you that her husband keeps a gun under the driver's seat and at various times when they are out he threatens her with the use of it, this law could fit that situation.

First and Second - Degree Recklessly Endangering Safety – 941.30

(1) Whoever recklessly endangers another's safety under circumstances which show utter disregard for human life is guilty of a Class F Felony.

(2) Second Degree - Whoever recklessly endangers another's safety is guilty of a Class G Felony.

So, Larry is in an argument with Lori and he is charging at her. Lori goes near the basement landing and she is holding their baby and Larry pushes her and their baby down the stairs. This charge would apply and voluntary intoxication is not a defense.

Opening Letters - 942.05

Whoever opens any sealed letter or package addressed to another, without the consent of the sender or the addressee, is guilty of a Class A Misdemeanor.

John's wife divorced him over an abusive relationship, and now John is curious what his ex-wife is up to. John knows what time her mail is delivered, and he sneaks to her mailbox and opens her letters every day.

Threats to Injure – 943.30(1)

Whoever, either verbally or by written or printed communication, maliciously threatens to accuse or accuses another of any crime or offense, or threatens or commits any injury to the person, property, business, profession, calling or trade, or the profits and income of any business, profession, calling or trade of another, with intent thereby to extort money or any pecuniary advantage whatever, or with intent to compel the person so threatened to do any act against the person's will or omit to do any lawful act, is guilty of a Class H Felony.

This may look confusing, and while it is classified as a property offense, it is adaptable as a domestic violence related charge if the abuser were to tell the victim, after an abuse situation, "If you tell anyone what happened here tonight, I'll break your arm!" Or, after hitting her, he tells his wife that if she reports this to the police, he will kill her.

Resisting or Obstructing Officer – 946.41

Whoever knowingly resists or obstructs an officer while such officer is doing an act in an official capacity and with lawful authority, is guilty of a Class A Misdemeanor.

So, when law enforcement shows up and the abuser lies about his name, or tries to mislead the officer, or puts up a struggle while the officers try to handcuff him, these charges would apply.

Escape – 946.42

If the officers have advised the defendant that he is under arrest for a crime and a reasonable person, under the circumstances as they existed, would have believed that he or she was not free to leave, and the defendant thereafter escapes, he or she can be charged with escape which is a Class H Felony under 946.42(3)(a).

Many abusers will try to make all kinds of excuses at the scene after law enforcement arrives in an attempt to minimize what happened and try to talk themselves out of the arrest. Things can change, though, when officers go to handcuff that person and many offenders take off running.

The Extortion Statute could also be used in the following way: I read in the paper recently that an adult son was asking his mom for money. She was elderly and what he would do is threaten her to give him $20,000 or he would kill her cat. Because she was alone and her cat was all that she had, she would give in and pay him because she really did believe that he would kill her pet. I don't know what the circumstances were in how this was reported to the police, but the son was arrested for extorting money from his mom.

Physical Abuse of a Child (Child Abuse) – 948.03

Intentional causation of bodily harm.

(2)(a) Whoever intentionally causes great bodily harm to a child is guilty of a Class E Felony.

(b) Whoever intentionally causes bodily harm to a child is guilty of a Class H Felony.

(c) Whoever intentionally causes bodily harm to a child by conduct which creates a high probability of great bodily harm is guilty of a Class F Felony.

In most homes that we respond to, where there is verbal, emotional, physical abuse to the mom, we usually find that the same abuse is and has been directed to the children in the home. We see children with huge bruises, fractures, belt marks or burn marks.

Sexual Assault of a Child – 948.02

There are varying degrees and the sad truth is that in some violent homes, there is also sexual abuse to the children.

Mistreating Animals – 951.02

No person may treat any animal, whether belonging to the person or another, in a cruel manner.

In many abusive homes, abusers are not only violent towards family, their violence can also turn to pets. Sometimes controllers even use threats of injury or death to pets to get their way.

Bailjumping – 946.49

If a defendant has been arrested and brought before a court commissioner or judge for a bond hearing or an initial appearance, the court will either impose a cash bond or a signature bond and after that the defendant can be released. The defendant will be subject to mandatory or discretionary conditions. All bonds require a defendant to appear for all scheduled court appearances, notify the clerk of court of any address change and prohibit the defendant from engaging in any further criminal activity. If the defendant violates any of these conditions, he/she will be arrested for bailjumping.

The court will also, in many cases, impose as a condition of bond that the defendant have no contact with the victim either by phone or in person. If the defendant has such a condition, and he goes to see the victim, he is violating the conditions of his bond which is bailjumping. The courts have recognized that these are dangerous situations for victims because most defendants, right after their release from jail, will start badgering the victim to convince her that she needs to go in and tell the court that nothing happened or that the injury was an accident. Sometimes victims are told to get a restraining order, which can also put the victim in harm's way from the abuser. By having the court impose the no contact order, it takes the burden away from the victim and still provides some safety.

If the original arrest involved alcohol, the court will oftentimes impose a "no taverns" or "no drink" order. So, if a defendant was intoxicated and battered his wife and restrained her from movement, and he was taken to jail on a battery charge and a Felony charge, and the next day he posts bond and is ordered to have no contact with the victim and to consume no alcohol, and the defendant goes directly home to confront the victim and has beer on his breath, and the police get called there, the defendant will be taken to jail and held on two Felony counts of bailjumping; one count for drinking and one for violating the no contact. This could expose the defendant (in Wisconsin) to ten years in prison, and if the defendant had been convicted recently for burglary, he is now facing 22 years in prison as he is a Felony repeater.

If the victim was very scared to proceed with the original battery charge and did start to recant, it doesn't matter now what the victim says or does as the defendant is now facing bailjumping charges.

Stalking – 940.32

There are cases when the victim is trying to get out of a dangerous relationship and the abuser will not leave her alone. The defendant may follow her everywhere that she goes and call her phone constantly. The abuser may send flowers to her work or force entry into her car and leave a card or rose taped to the steering wheel. The stalker may even flatten her car tires or pour substances into her gas tank. In Wisconsin, a course of conduct means two or more acts, carried out over time, however short or long, that show a continuity of purpose, including any of the following:

Maintaining a visual or physical proximity to the victim.

Approaching or confronting the victim.

Appearing at the victim's workplace or contacting the victim's employer or co-workers.

Appearing at the victim's home or contacting the victim's neighbors.

Entering property owned, leased or occupied by the victim.

Contacting the victim by telephone or causing the victim's telephone or any other person's phone to ring repeatedly or continuously, whether conversation takes place or not.

Photographing, videotaping, audio taping, or through any other electronic means, monitoring or recording the activities of the victim.

Sending material by any means to the victim or, for the purpose of obtaining information about, disseminating information about, or communicating with the victim, to a member of the victim's family or household or an employer, co-worker or friend of the victim.

Placing an object on or delivering an object to property owned, leased or occupied by the victim.

Delivering an object to a member of the victim's family or an employer, co-worker or friend of the victim or placing an object on, or delivering an object to, property owned, leased or occupied by such a person with the intent that the object be delivered to the victim.

Causing a person to engage in any of these previously listed acts.

An actor then is guilty of a Class I Felony if:

"The actor intentionally engages in a course of conduct directed at a specific person that would cause a reasonable person under the same circumstances to suffer serious emotional distress or to fear bodily injury to or death of himself or herself or a member of his or her family or household.

The actor knows or should know that at least one of the acts that constitute the course of conduct will cause the specific person to suffer serious emotional distress or place the specific person in a reasonable fear of bodily injury to or the death of himself, herself or a member of his or her family or household.

There are also higher penalties for repeat offenders of Stalking.

Remember, not all stalkers kill the person they are stalking, but most stalking victims are killed by their stalkers. These are very dangerous situations and can easily involve your church.

Rachel has two kids and brings them to church with her every Sunday. Rachel has told her pastor that her estranged husband has been following her everywhere, and today she has just dropped off her kids at their Sunday School classes, and she fears that Ron will show up today and either sit in the pew behind her or possibly take the kids and leave while she is in the service.

There have been many cases across the country in recent years where an abuser has shown up at church and shot and killed the victim and other congregation members, including the pastor.

Churches are not very good at safety planning when they become aware of such situations. Churches will often be very reluctant to call the police or sheriff to report a stalking person sitting in the church parking lot, or sitting outside of someone's home during a midweek church small group gathering at someone's home.

Churches need to be less concerned about what it looks like to neighbors or other congregation members and be willing to call law enforcement. If the church leadership is aware of a volatile situation where the stalker may come in and try to cause a scene or take the children from their Sunday School classes, they need to have a plan. The class teachers should be made aware and told to not release the children to anyone but their mother. Greeters may have to be posted at the church doors throughout the service with the church doors locked. They can allow in those who are late and not let the abuser in. They should be told to dial 9-1-1 immediately if the suspect stalker shows up.

And all of this can be done without making the entire congregation aware and without causing a great deal of disruption if it is planned out correctly.

Violations of Probation and Parole

Not everyone convicted in a domestic violence case goes to jail. Many times the court may offer probation as long as the defendant does not consume alcohol, does not have contact with the victim, and attends some sort of anger management training or other counseling. The defendant is also assigned a probation agent whom he/she must check in with on a regular basis. Any violations of the conditions of probation could land the actor in jail, and could lead to the revocation of the probation which means the abuser would have to serve the jail time that was stayed by the judge in lieu of a chance at being placed on probation. So it is very important to report any violations to law enforcement immediately.

This chapter dealt with laws that we have at our disposal to deal with domestic violence. These laws protect victims, and at the same time hold the abuser ACCOUNTABLE for their actions. A clear message needs to be sent to abusers that what they are doing is wrong. The victim needs to hear that he or she does not need to put up with violence and threats.

Chapter Three

How Does Abuse Happen?

BLANCHE STARTED HER DAY LIKE any other day. She picked up around the house, made the bed, did a load of laundry and she just finished loading the dishwasher. Ralph is at work and she has a few errands to run later today, but for right now Blanche is going to sit down in the kitchen and read the paper with a cup of coffee. Blanche looks outside and sees the beautiful colors as the leaves are changing. Today is October 17th, and right now Blanche doesn't even know that it is Domestic Violence Awareness Month. Before today, she didn't even know such a month existed. Blanche glances through the paper and an ad on page five catches her attention. The ad was placed there by the local Domestic Violence advocacy group in town, and it proclaims that October is Domestic Violence Awareness Month, and the ad lists certain behaviors that could be an indication that a person lives in an abusive relationship. The ad further lists the services that they offer, including counseling and a shelter to take in and temporarily house victims of domestic abuse.

As Blanche reads the ad, she feels her hands tremble, and she even spills coffee on her new white table cloth. She feels her knees knock, her pulse is racing, and she can hardly catch her breath. Blanche tears the ad out of the paper, folds it in half and places it into her purse. She runs to her bedroom, grabs a small suitcase, throws in several changes of clothes. She grabs her most expensive jewelry and puts that into the case. She grabs some bank papers and credit card statements and drives straight to the abuse shelter.

Blanche is met at the door by an advocate there, tears are streaming down her face. She cannot control her trembling and shaking, and the advocate greets her kindly, welcomes her in and has her sit down. The advocate asks her her name and she replies, "Bbblance, my name is Blanche." The advocate can tell that Blanche is quite shaken and asks why she is here. Blanche explains that she thinks that she lives in an abusive home and says that she didn't even realize how bad it was, "Until I saw this today in the paper." Blanche's hand shakes as she reaches into her purse and pulls out the ad. The advocate says, "Oh, our ad, that just ran today. What makes you say that you live in an abusive relationship?" Blanche is looking down, picking her nails and she can't even get the words out. The advocate asks, "Are you beaten or shoved?" Blanche says, "No, nothing like that." "Well, have you ever been injured?" Blanche, still shaking says, "Yes." "O.K., was it last week? Or last month?" Blanche says, "No, nothing real recent." The advocate asks, "Are you yelled at a lot or called names?" Blanche shakes her head no. "Well, then," (the advocate asks), "how long ago were you injured?'" Blanche replies, "It's been 24 years, 11 months and about 10 days." "Well, why don't you tell me about it," the advocate says as she reaches out to take Blanche's hand.

Blanche takes three really deep breaths and begins, "You know, I've never told this story to anyone, not one soul." Blanche starts to shake and cry some more, takes another deep breath and then says, "It was about two weeks after Ralph and I were married, he was always so calm and caring, and one day, it was a Saturday, and if you asked me why we were arguing I swear to God that I don't even remember what the fight was about. But just then Ralph had this angry look on his face, he screamed at me like no one has ever screamed before. Ralph charged at me, I was up against the wall in the kitchen, the basement door was open, and he was so mad he swore at me and then shoved me. Well, I flew right down the basement stairs, every step down I tried to put my hands up over my head. I thought to myself, if I can just protect my head maybe I won't die – I really thought I would die. I thought for sure that I was a goner. I know that I blacked out and I don't even know for how long. When I did come to, Ralph, the same man who used those hands to attack me and push me, were now softly caressing my forehead with one hand and the other was gently holding a wet rag on my left ear, which had blood pouring out of it. I'm sure I had broken a rib or two, my head swelled up like a basketball and I couldn't walk or use my arms for weeks, maybe a month. I told Ralph that I needed to go to the hospital and he changed from the warm caregiver to the angry man who had just attacked me. He gritted his teeth and said, 'Absolutely not! You can't go to the emergency room like this, what will they ask? What would you tell them? What could happen? I will care for you, I will be your nurse and you'll be O.K. I'm sorry that I did this, I don't know what came over me.'

Well, Ralph brought a twin mattress from the spare room down to the basement and that's where I stayed for about two weeks. I was in such pain, I still thought that I would die. I had no phone and he wouldn't bring one down to me. Whenever my sister would call, I could hear him upstairs telling her that I was either out shopping or laying down taking a nap. He was eventually able to help me up the stairs and I could see that I was getting better. I felt that I should just keep my mouth shut about the whole thing and he kept apologizing and he would bring me flowers. Somehow I thought that this was just a huge, tragic mistake and that things would get better. And the strange thing was that things did get better. Ralph hardly argued with me and took good care of me.

"Finally, after about four months, I still had some slight pain now and again, but I was just about back to normal. Then one day Ralph was sitting in his chair, smoking his pipe and reading the paper, and I disagreed with a decision of his, and when I started to explain my view, very calmly, never raising his voice, just turning a page and never looking up at me, he asked me, 'Blanche, how would you like to take another trip down the stairs?' Well, I shut up, I gave in, and almost every month since that day, whenever I voice my opinion or try to share a concern, he very calmly and quietly asks me the same thing and I just shut up and shut down. We just had a disagreement about an upcoming vacation destination, and just last week in the middle of the conversation he looked down, then pointed to the basement door and in a quiet tone asked, 'Now, Blanche, you wouldn't want to go for another trip down the stairs, would you?'"

People often ask victims of domestic violence what is going on, they ask what happened to you today or last week. We need to understand that while there may be a span of time in the actual abuse (just in Blanche's case), it is the on-going effect that the original incident had on the victim that controls how they feel.

So, we have to ask ourselves: How does abuse occur? How does it start? Is it a taught behavior or a learned behavior?

Violent behaviors can be taught. I have arrested abusers who have told me that their dad did the same thing to their mom when they were growing up. Some abusers have told me that it is their right and duty to make sure that their wife learns to respect them and they feel perfectly justified in their abusive actions. These men will say that domestic violence laws are government interfering in the private affairs of families.

Other men that I have arrested have also said that their father abused their mother, and they may say, "And I always swore to myself that I would never do the same thing to my wife if I ever got married, and just look at me, look what I've become, look what I did to my wife tonight!"

My friend, Gregg Janicek, a retired Wisconsin Probation and Parole Agent, who has spent years working with convicted abusers, explained to me the following, which shows how abuse can be a learned behavior. Let's look at Tony and Bev, who were just married three weeks ago. One day Bev notices that Tony's clothes are just piling up on the floor in their bedroom. Bev can't even tell what is dirty and which clothes are clean because Tony never puts anything away. So, Bev calls Tony in from the garage and she says, "Tony dear, I always grew up in a neat and tidy home, and even when I went away to college, my dorm room was spotless. I really need you to not pile up your clothes like this. After all, you never know when company may stop by." In a normal, healthy relationship Tony responds by saying, "Gee, Bev, I guess I'm kind of a slob and I didn't realize that this bothered you. I'm sorry, and I will do my best to make sure that it doesn't happen again." And the truth is that it may happen again, but because they have a mutual understanding and the ability to work things out, the problem will eventually correct itself.

The graph on this page represents 25 years of marriage for Tony and Bev. Each little bump on the line represents a small argument or disagreement and an issue, and they are small bumps because of the oneness, and the desire of each to communicate, understand and work through each difficulty that comes along during their lives.

1 ~~~~~~~~~~~~~~~~~~~~~~~ 25

Now, let's look at Tony and Bev in an unhealthy relationship. Bev notices that Tony's clothes are all piled up in the bedroom and she calls him in, points out the problem, tells him that she has always had a neat and tidy home, and she asks him to clean it up and to pledge to put things away. Tony picks up the things, says that he is sorry and tells her that it will never happen again. But, the next week, Bev is a bit frustrated when she notices that the clothes are piling up again. So, Bev calls Tony in from the garage and says, "Gee, Tony, you know we just talked about this last week, and here your clothes are, all piled up on the floor again." Tony takes a deep sigh, rolls his eyes and maybe says, "I know, I know, O.K., I'll pick them up."

Another week goes by and Bev notices that the clothes are piling up again all over the floor and she calls for Tony, who is out in the front yard replacing the line on the weed eater. She says, "Tony, this clothes thing is really upsetting me and I need you to quit throwing things all over the floor." Tony rolls his eyes again and says, "Bev, you're just like my mother, always nagging me about something!"

Bev takes offense to that and says, "I'm not nagging, I'm just trying to get you to see that what you are doing is bothering me." Then it happens, Tony is angry, and he takes his right hand and slams it on the wall so hard that the pictures shake. At the same time with his left index finger in Bev's face he screams, "YOU ARE NAGGING ME, NOW LEAVE ME ALONE!!" Well, Bev jumped backwards when he hit the wall. "Where did that come from?" she asks herself, and she is so startled and scared, she jumped backwards about two feet. She then says nothing. She just quietly walks out of the room, and for the first time in their married life she is actually scared to be with her own husband. This is where the "walking on eggshells" part comes in. Bev now learned that she better be careful what she says as she is afraid to confront Tony now. Bev spends three weeks not saying a word about the clothes, which continue to pile up and she has resorted to just picking them up herself.

Tony learned something, too. Tony learned that violence works. He learned that after he scared her like that, that she shut up, she not only quit asking him to change his ways, but he notices that she is even picking up his things for him.

Well, like most people, Bev can only be silent for so long, and about a month later she is tired of not feeling free to express how she feels and she grows resentful that she has to pick up his things as there has been no change on Tony's part. So, Bev confronts Tony again, and this time he slams his hand on the kitchen counter real hard and yells at her, "YOU BETTER QUIT TELLING ME WHAT TO DO!!" Bev is startled again and just shuts her mouth and quietly walks away. Tony learns, again, that this stuff works, it shuts her up, and it shuts her up for a month or so, rather than him having to hear anything every other day. But at what price? Their closeness and intimacy is drying up, Bev is scared and confused and can't believe that she never "picked up" on his violent side before they were married and, in their case, Tony never exhibited a violent or abusive side while he and Bev were dating.

Bev keeps quiet another month, the clothes are still piling up and she is still picking up after Tony. Again, she feels that she can no longer keep silent and she confronts Tony again. And, same as last time, Tony pounds his fist on the table, but he notices something. Bev is not shutting up, she is staying right in there telling him how she feels. You see, at some point she became desensitized to the slamming of the hand or fist, and it no longer startles her or stops her in her tracks like it did the first two times. So, Tony feels this loss of power and control and he decides to pick up a plate and toss it across the room. It hits the wall and smashes into tiny pieces. Now, this gets Bev's attention. She is now zipping her lip and walking away, just shocked, startled and even more afraid than she was before. And Tony has learned that his violent outbursts work, for a while, and that he may have to step it up a notch from time to time to maintain the control that he had. Over time, this escalation leads to pushing, shoving, slapping, hitting and many of the other crimes that we looked at in Chapter Two.

If you look at the graph below, it, too, represents 25 years of marriage in this unhealthy relationship. Like the line in the healthy relationship, it started out with just a few, teeny, tiny bumps which were the very first disagreements which were originally dealt with in a loving, caring and understanding way. The big spikes that you see are the major flare ups that resulted in some form of abuse or violence. The left side of the spike is the escalation that led to the slamming of the hand or the throwing of the plate. The tip of the spike is the actual act of violence that occurred, and the down slope of the spike is when Bev just shut up and walked away. It also represents a making up period, as most victims have told me that the abusing spouse usually felt bad after the incident and made some form of an apology. But you will notice that the line stemming from the flare up goes up a notch, because the relationship can never be the same. That violent episode is forever etched in the mind of the victim. The lines leading up to the next spike are the "walking on eggshells" periods where there are no disagreements because the victim learns to keep quiet and not say anything as the victim fears what will happen next.

As each spike occurs, they get bigger because the level of violence becomes bigger and uglier.

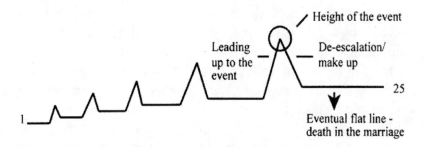

Lack of wanting to communicate or avoidance of a confrontation can also lead to an abusive episode. Jerry bought a new rifle two months ago and has never had a chance to sight it in and do some practice shooting with it. Deer hunting season is just a month away and his friend from work invited Jerry to go to the shooting range this Saturday. Jerry doesn't dare ask Carm if he can go to the hunt club. He has a whole list of things at home that need to be done, and he fears that if he says he is going to the range she will get angry. So, Jerry picks an argument about some little, insignificant matter and escalates and escalates until he is calling her names and slamming doors. Finally, Carm just yells, "That's it! Just get out of the house!" And with that permission to leave, Jerry takes off and goes to the range with his friend. It worked. He got to do what he wanted to do, however at what price? There are still the hurt feelings and Carm's total disillusionment about what just happened, because she can't understand why that conversation just turned out the way it did. What she does not know is that it was planned out to go that way by Jerry.

Now, I use Jerry as the one who started the argument to get his way, and some people will say that women can do the same thing to men. This is true, and as I stated in the beginning of the book, women and men are both capable of being abusers. Statistics show us, though, that in a vast majority of cases the woman is the victim of the abuse.

When I have talked to abusers, they will either say that nothing happened ("My wife fell," or "She got in the way of the beer bottle I threw across the room") or they will say, "I don't know what happened to me, I just lost control." But WHO did the abuser lose control over? The abuser lost control over the victim, got mad, escalated and then acted out in a violent way. Most abusers will tell you that they would never dream of acting the way they did at home to their spouse to anyone at work. And if you ask them why, they will tell you that at work they would be fired. An abuser in the checkout at a grocery store may roll his eyes and be angry if the person in front of them has 24 items in the "20 Items or Less" checkout line, but he would never dream of lashing out at or pushing or hitting the customer in front of them. Why? Because most will tell you that if the same episode at home was played out in public, someone would call the police and they would be arrested.

While abusers may have anger issues and may benefit from anger management counseling, for the most part they can control their anger at home, they just choose not to. And most abusers do not want anyone to know that they are abusing their spouse. They know what their neighbors, co-workers and friends would think of them if these other people knew what the abuser was doing to a spouse. In most homes, it's the "family secret" that no one is allowed to talk about. Most victims in abusive relationships have no one to confide in and, even if they did, they have been told by the abuser not to tell anyone what happened. When others find out that a friend or relative is being abused, people tend to ask the victim why she stays or why she had never told anyone. Most victims will tell you that all it takes is to be strangled once, and when you see that the abuser is capable of determining whether you live or die, you learn real quick to keep quiet. We will discuss later why victims stay in abusive relationships, but right now we are talking about why the abuser abuses.

It's the night before Easter Sunday and Sandra goes to Darrin and asks him for money to buy Easter baskets for the kids. It's 9:30 at night and she has been asking him all day. Darrin is drunk, he is frantically working on the State and Federal tax forms because he put it off all spring, and he even has a two day reprieve from the government because the 15th fell on a Saturday. Every time she asks him, he gets more irate and finally he throws his pen at her and says, "For the last time! No!" And it isn't like he doesn't have money for her to buy Easter baskets, he just doesn't want to spend the money. So, Sandra goes to him one last time and asks for some money to go buy some cigarettes. He slams his hand down on the table and says, "No! I'm not giving you any money! Now leave me alone!" Beer cans are stacked in pyramids all around the house. Some are hers, some are his. She, too, has resorted to drinking as an escape from the daily horrors that she faces because she, too, says that she "walks around on eggshells."

This night, though, Sandra has had it. Darrin never gives her any money for anything, and she is not allowed to have a job. Darrin has told her that a woman's place is in the home, and if she worked she wouldn't have dinner ready when he comes home from work. Sandra stands next to him at the receipt and tax form filled kitchen table and says, "Darrin, it just isn't fair. I don't know of any other wife who gets treated like this. I'm tired of always having to run to you for money and you usually tell me no. I saw a sign in the window at the gas station the other day, they are looking for a part-time clerk, in the morning, way before you would come home. It won't interfere with anything, I promise." Darrin, looks up and screams, "How am I going to get these taxes done if you don't leave me alone!!!" He stands up and kicks his chair backwards and it hits the sliding glass door so hard Sandra thought it would break for sure. Darrin continues, "We have had this conversation a hundred times, and I distinctly recall telling you the last time that you brought it up to NEVER bring it up again. That's final, you are not going to get a job! You can't even keep this dump cleaned up, just look at this place!!" Sandra starts to cry and whimpers, "It just isn't fair, it isn't fair to the kids. They are going to be looking around for a basket tomorrow and are you going to be the one to tell them that they got nothing?" Darrin growls, "THEY ARE 9 AND 11! I THINK THEY'VE OUTGROWN THE WHOLE EASTER BUNNY GIG, SO GET OVER IT!!" "Well," Sandra says as she walks away, "I am going to look into that job. I just think a little extra spending money wouldn't hurt either one of us." Darrin comes up behind Sandra real fast, grabs her pony tail and throws her to the floor. Sandra's glasses break and she is bleeding from the side of her face which hit the edge of the wooden molding at the bottom of the cabinet. Her left arm and hip hurt because she landed on her side. Darrin is just standing over her, yelling and screaming at her, telling her that no wife of his is going to have a job, and that he is the man, he makes the decisions, and this decision is final. "YOU ARE NOT GETTING A JOB, NOT NOW, NOT EVER! AND DON'T YOU EVEN THINK OF EVER ASKING ME ABOUT IT AGAIN!!"

I have told this story to several "church going" people and the response I usually get is: "Why did she want to buy cigarettes? Doesn't she know they are bad for you? Hasn't she ever read in the Bible that our bodies are a temple? Some way to treat a temple."

And this is one of the huge problems in churches today. We are not sensitive to victims of abuse, we gloss over the main, real problem and focus on one small part of the story that may go against what we feel is right. Don't miss the point. The point is that Sandra could have asked Darrin for money to go buy a pack of gum and the answer would have been no. Darrin is using male privilege to control Sandra. He treats her like a servant, he is the final authority in defining the roles of a wife and a husband. He is using economic abuse against her by refusing to let her get a job, making her ask for money (and then not letting her have any) for things that he will not let her buy, just because he wants to be the one to make all decisions.

Darrin was arrested and taken to jail and, as it turns out, Darrin has had some exposure to church, because on the way to jail he told me how wrong I was to arrest HIM, and that the Bible says that, "The wife must submit to her husband." I asked him what that meant and he got mad and said, "Well, you obviously don't go to church, but it means that I'm in charge and she's nothing." I had never told him anything about my religious beliefs, but this isn't an uncommon thing, because many abusers that go to jail start quoting scripture in a vast majority of calls that I've been on.

So, I glanced over my right shoulder, looking at Darrin through the cage of my squad car and said, "Well, congratulations." "For what?" he mumbled back, and I said, "For being in charge of nothing," I replied. Darrin sat up fast with his shoulders back and said, "Just what do you mean by that?" And I told him that by using male privilege to control every aspect of his wife's life he has reduced her to nothing. Well, he got very angry and said that I needed to go to church so that I could learn what he was talking about. He went on to say, "It's always supposed to have been like that, my mom was never allowed to work, she had to stay home, and so did my grandma. And if you don't like it, too bad!"

Linda and Chad just got a divorce two months ago. Everything was finalized except for one thing, they are still living together. The house is not on the market because of damaged doors and numerous holes in the wall. Chad keeps saying that he is going to repair things, and will not allow Linda to call a realtor until he makes the repairs. Linda knows that Chad is lazy and does not think he will ever fix these things. She doesn't know how to, she doesn't have the money to hire a handyman, and even if she did, Chad would never allow it. Linda has even thought of putting the house on the market "as is," but Chad would become enraged if she called a realtor on her own because he has told her, "I make all the decisions!"

The whole thing started about six months ago. While the abuse had gone on for most of their 17 years of marriage, it really came to a head two days before Christmas last year. Linda works, "Against my better judgment," says Chad, and two days before Christmas, someone at work suggested that everyone from her department go out for a little office party. They all went to a restaurant, ate and afterwards they stayed in the bar area and visited for a while. The day that Linda found out about the party she told Chad and he blew up and said, "Absolutely not! You are not going to that party!" Well, Linda decided that she likes these people at work, they treat her way better than her own husband does, and what could be the harm in visiting with and being a part of something at work? So, Linda went. Well, the whole time she was there her cell phone rang about 20 different times. It was Chad, sitting at home. He was drunk and screaming at her to come home and, "Why would you go somewhere after I told you that you couldn't go?!" Linda was embarrassed because all of her co-workers, who were having fun and visiting with one another, kept glancing over at Linda because they could tell that she was in distress.

Linda even left early and came home. The minute she walked in the door Chad jumped up from his chair, he attacked her, pinned her up against the wall. He had his right forearm on her throat, she couldn't breath, she couldn't move, she couldn't believe that this was happening to her. Chad threw her to the ground, kicked her in the stomach. Linda curled up into a ball and he kicked her back and buttocks, and the whole time he was screaming and swearing at her. Then Chad picked up a hammer that was on the kitchen counter and pinned Linda up against the wall again. He then swung the hammer at her head, and at the last second he moved the hammer to the right and struck the wall. Linda thought she was a goner for sure. He slapped her face, threw her to the ground and then went around the house slamming the hammer into all of the walls and doors throughout the home. He knocked over lamps, broke vases. He was on a wild rampage. A neighbor who had let his dog outside heard the shouting, the crying and heard the loud banging sounds coming from their house. The neighbor called 9-1-1 and said that he wasn't sure what was going on next door, "But you better hurry, it sounds really bad."

Two officers arrived, they walked up to the house and heard the screaming, pounding and the cries of a woman saying, "No, please stop this!" The officers saw that the door was open about an inch, so they walked in. Just as the officers stepped into the tri-level home, they jumped back just in time as to their amazement they saw an entertainment center with a television on it being shoved over the railing of the living room just above them. The T.V. smashed to the floor, and they ran up the stairs and Chad now charged at them. They had radioed for backup officers and ended up pepper spraying Chad. They were able to subdue him and get him handcuffed. Chad was taken to jail and had a bunch of charges on him. He called Linda from jail and vowed to pay her back "big time" once he was out of jail. Chad did get out of jail, the abuse continued, he was found guilty of the charges and he was placed on probation.

Chad told her, "That's it! We are done!" and Chad retained his lawyer to proceed with a divorce. Linda and Chad's divorce was finalized four months later and, to this day, because they couldn't sell the house, they have been stuck here, still living in the house together. Neither can afford to move on until the proceeds of the house sale are divided.

So tonight, Linda is getting ready to do her paper route. In order to have more money, she took on this paper route which starts every day at 2:30 a.m. The paper bundles are dropped off in her driveway, she drags them into the house, she folds them into threes, puts a rubber band around them, puts them into a clothes basket and then carries them out to her minivan. She went to start her van and nothing, the van wouldn't start. She goes back into the house, wakes up Chad and asks if he can jump start her van. "Don't bother me!! Get out!!" Chad snaps at her. "But Chad, what will I do, I have to deliver these, can I use your car?" "How does it feel to want?" Chad yelled back. "You're on your own now, you're the one who wanted to do your own thing, so go figure it out!" Linda started to cry and said, "Please Chad, I beg of you, if I don't deliver these I'll get fired." "Do you know how pathetic you sound? Here's a grown woman, 48 years old, afraid she's gonna get fired from a paper route!" Chad just laughs in her face. Linda asks to use his car once more and Chad jumps off of the couch, knocks her to the ground, pulls her back up, and now he is strangling her with both hands around her throat. Linda reaches to her right, grabs the phone and she manages to dial 9-1-1. "9-1-1 operator, what is your emergency?" a voice comes over the phone. Chad hears that, grabs the phone, disconnects the call and punches Linda in the stomach for having placed that call.

Officers are sent to the home because, while the operator never spoke to anyone, she did hear a male voice screaming. Officers arrive and

Chad answers the door. He is calm and says, "Hi officers, what's the problem?" "Why don't you tell us," the one officer replies. "Someone here just dialed 9-1-1." Well, yes, we are sorry, we were trying to make a call that starts with a 9-1-4 and we must have hit the 1 twice." "Well, our dispatcher heard yelling and is this your wife?" "Ex-wife!" Chad interrupts. The officer continues. "She looks sad like she's been crying." Linda is standing behind Chad and she is motioning with her hands around her throat and then pointing to Chad. The one officer sees this and tells Chad, "Well, we have a few questions for you. We just need to make sure that everything is fine, could you step outside and talk to my partner a minute. Chad walks outside and just then Linda trembles and is shaking, her voice is like a whisper because she was just strangled, and she tells the officer everything that happened and why she was unable to talk to the dispatcher. The officers go outside and arrest Chad.

He is violating his probation from the first incident by drinking and because he was ordered by the judge to not engage in any further violent situations. He is also charged now with substantial battery and disorderly conduct. The officer who was talking to Linda is finishing up with some paperwork with her when she says, "This is just all of my fault, my whole life is ruined, and it's all my fault." The officer while writing glances up and asks, "What's your fault?" "Well, just everything," Linda replies. "If I hadn't gone to that stupid work party for Christmas none of this would have ever happened." The officer she was talking to had not responded to that past call, and while he did see the holes everywhere, she filled him in on everything that had happened. The officer said to Linda, "Well, I don't understand, are you not free to do what you want to do?" Linda said, "Well, no, I guess he just prefers me to do what he tells me to do." She continued, "Chad just wants to know where I am, and if he does not agree, he get's mad. It was just a party, and my husband told me, he warned me not to go and I shouldn't have." The officer said, "That is crazy, how could any of this be your fault? It sounds like Chad is a controller." "What's that you say?" Linda asked, "A controller?" "Yes," the officer said, "a controller."

The officer continued, "There are women that we deal with who have husbands or boyfriends who totally dominate and dictate everything that their wife or girlfriend does. Would you believe that some of these guys follow them around, check their odometers, check their e-mails, voice mails, everything, because they feel that they have this right, this privilege to do these things?" Linda just sat there, shaking and crying and said, "He's done all of those things to me, the whole time that we have been together. He always tells me that the man is in control and the woman is supposed to obey and do as she is told. Even his dad and grandfather acted like that."

When I was little we would go visit my Aunt Eve and Uncle Walter once a month. They lived about an hour and a half away and they had no kids. It was 1975, I was 12, my older brother was 14, and I had a younger sister and a younger brother who were also two years apart in age. We dreaded going. Not that we didn't like to visit my Aunt Eve; she was a sweet lady who would do anything for anyone. But my Uncle Walter was very cross and always in a bad mood. My mom would spend most of her time in the kitchen helping my aunt while us four kids sat in the livingroom with my dad and our uncle.

Uncle Walter didn't get out of his chair for anything. If he was drinking a lemonade, when his glass was empty he would raise it up and shake it so hard that the ice cubes would make a loud jingling noise. That was my aunt's cue to drop whatever she was doing and come running into the living room to retrieve his glass, refill it and get it back to him "ASAP." And, if for some reason she didn't hear the ice cubes jingling, he would let out repeated yells of "EVE! EVE!" He would become very angry if he had to call her name because, after all, to him she should have heard the ice the first time.

My aunt worked part time. And the only reason that she was "allowed" to have employment outside of the home was because it was at their local high school and she worked in the cafeteria, and every day she got to take home the leftovers which my uncle would scarf down.

Our visits consisted of my dad and uncle arguing about politics, or the Viet Nam War, or something. No matter what the topic, my uncle would take the opposing view and spend hours arguing. When he ate dinner, my uncle never engaged in conversation; he would eat quickly, then move to his chair and continue to watch T.V. My mom and aunt would then do all of the dishes while we had the enjoyment of listening to my uncle continue to bark out orders to our aunt, usually during the commercials of his favorite T.V. shows. First, there was the "Lawrence Welk Show" (which was very exciting for four kids), followed by "Hee Haw" (another exciting show), and then "All In The Family," and it was hard to keep a straight face as my older brother and me would point with our index finger of our left hand at our uncle (we blocked the pointing with our right hand) every time that Archie Bunker would say something. It was amazing. On the way home I would tell my mom, "Our Uncle Walter is Archie Bunker."

My grandma was my Aunt Eve's sister, and I asked my grandma one day, "Why does Uncle Walter treat Aunt Eve like that?" "Well," she said, "he's just like that, he always has been. We all warned her that he was a rough person, but your Aunt Eve thought she could change him." My grandma continued, "Plus, he grew up in that generation, that's how it's been." Well, I didn't understand what that meant, but I do know that they grew old and died very unhappy people.

Ben and Ally just got married and Ben told her, "Now, let's get one thing straight. The man's job is to do all of the outside work. I'll mow the lawn, trim the bushes, edge the grass and clear the driveway when it snows. The woman's job is the inside stuff, vacuuming, laundry, dishes, dusting. Any questions?" Well, Ally didn't know what to ask or say, so she said, "O.K." And Ben added one more thing. "Oh, and cooking, you cook, I don't know how to." Well, this arrangement worked for a few weeks and Ally became increasingly bitter. She was discovering that Ben's outside work detail took about two hours a week as he mowed the lawn every Saturday from about 11:00 in the morning until about 1:00 in the afternoon. She also noticed that his work looked more like fun, as he usually spent half an hour of that time talking to the neighbor guy who was also out working in his yard.

So, as Ally stood at the sink scraping dried cereal from Ben's bowl that he had never rinsed out, she said to herself, "I have to talk to Ben." "Ben, can you come in here for a minute please?" Ben came in from the living room and Ally said, "You know, this whole me doing the inside work and you doing the lawn isn't working for me. This isn't what I signed up for when I married you and I think you need to step up and help me. This is so much work, and look at us, it's just the two of us. Can you imagine how hard this is going to get when we have kids?" Ben was getting mad and said, "Well, you'll have to manage it, this is how it is, like it or not." "But Ben," Ally said, "I didn't grow up like this. There were five of us kids and when my dad came home from work he rolled up his sleeves and helped fold clothes, he did dishes, he cooked, he did whatever was needed." Ben replied, "Well, that's his problem. I run things like my dad. He told me that it's always been like this and this is the way it's supposed to be. Even God made Eve for Adam to be his helper, says so in the Bible."

What Ben is referencing here is Genesis 2:20 "But for Adam no suitable helper was found." (New International Version.) And in the King James Version we read "...but for Adam there was not found a help mate for him." Did Eve just arrive to come and take care of Adam and be a subservient doormat? I don't think so. In fact, this word helper is used by the Hebrews writer in Hebrews 13:6 (NIV), "So we can say in confidence, 'The Lord is my helper; I will not be afraid. What can man do to me?'" And it reads in the KJV, "So that we may boldly say, 'The Lord is my helper, and I will not fear what man shall do unto me.'" Does Ben actually believe then that God, as described in Hebrews is his personal subservient doormat at his beck and call? Absolutely not. Ally is a co-heir in the Kingdom of Christ, she's a sister in Christ, and he is to love and cherish her. Ally is not less important just because she may not have the exact same role as Ben. Ally was never created to just be a person who helps out and assists Ben in everything that HE wants. The Hebrews writer is a person who realizes that he has big problems and lots of trouble in his life, and he can't help himself. He really needs God to hear him and to respond with some help. If Ben's comparison of the "helper" of Eve and the "helper" in Hebrews is the same, he doesn't understand that God never created Eve to be a subservient doormat, just as much as God is not a subservient doormat for us.

The way that this story ends is not uncommon. One day Ally gets so sick and tired of the situation that she announces, "I'm on strike, let the dishes pile up." And Ben responds with, "O.K., well, I'm on strike, too, let the grass get knee high." Next, the two are no longer talking to one another, and then one is sleeping on the couch. Because no one will bend or give in, and no one will do anything, they are making separate meals and eating off of paper plates. Things escalate and abuse often follows. I have seen this played out in so many calls that I have responded to.

So, how did people get this idea that "the man rules" or "my wife is supposed to cater to me?" Some people will argue that at one point in history there was a "Rule of Thumb," and this rule was that a man could not hit his wife with a stick that was wider than his thumb when he held it in his hand. Now, some people will argue that there was no English Common Law that ever approved of a "Rule of Thumb," however we can take a look at history and see that the courts and society attitudes have encouraged the belief of the predominance of a husband over his wife.

Bradley v. State, 1824, a judge acknowledges the existence of a thumb standard but rejects it as justification in this case. A decision by the Mississippi Supreme Court in this case allows a husband to administer only a "moderate chastisement in cases of emergency."

1829, in England, a husband's absolute power of chastisement against his wife is abolished.

1866, The American Society for the Prevention of Cruelty to Animals is founded. It comes before the Society for Prevention of Cruelty to Children in 1875, and there was no such organization devoted to the awareness or prevention of cruelty to women. It is also interesting that today there are 4,000 animal shelters nationwide and only 1,000 protection shelters for women. Animals are important to protect, but so are humans. I can remember a call at the police department a few years back when a guy beat a dog to the point that it was bleeding. The story made the front page, and our dispatch center was flooded with calls from citizens who wanted to know when the defendant's court date was so they could show up and make sure that justice was served. That same week we had a baby born at home, and the mother who did not want to keep it, threw her newborn in the trash. The week after that, a woman in a nearby city was shot to death by her husband. No one called asking what their court dates were. There were no protests, no public outrage.

In 1867, a man in North Carolina was acquitted of striking his wife three times with a stick about the size of one of his fingers, but smaller than his thumb. The appellate court later upheld the acquittal on the grounds that the court "should not interfere with family government in trifling cases."

1871, Alabama is the first state to rescind the legal right of men to beat their wives in *Fugraham v. State*. Massachusetts also declares wife beating illegal.

1874, the "finger switch" rule is put down when the Supreme Court of North Carolina rules that "the husband has no right to chastise his wife under any circumstances." The court further ruled: "If no permanent injury has been inflicted, nor malice, cruelty, nor dangerous violence shown by the husband, it is better to draw the curtain, shut out the public gaze and leave the parties to forgive and forget."

1878, Francis Power Cobbe published "Wife Torture in England." She brought to light the treatment of wives in Liverpool's "Kicking District." She documented 6,000 of the worst assaults on women over a three year period. Some were maimed, blinded, burned and some murdered. Cobbe's belief was that the abuse occurred because of the popular belief that a man's wife was his property. Men in Parliament passed the Matrimonial Causes Act which allowed victims of violence to obtain a legal separation from the abusing husband. It gave the wife the right to have custody of the children, a right to property and earnings. A separation could only occur if the husband had been convicted of aggravated assault and if the court believed that she was in grave danger.

1880s in England, the law changes to allow a wife to separate, but not divorce if she is habitually beaten by her husband to the point of "endangering her life."

1882, Maryland is the first state to pass a law that makes wife beating a crime punishable by forty lashes or a year in jail.

1886, a lower court in North Carolina rules that a criminal indictment cannot be brought against a husband unless the battery is so severe that "it results in permanent injury, endangers life and limb, or is malicious beyond reasonable grounds."

1890, the North Carolina Supreme Court prohibits a husband from committing even a slight assault on his wife.

August 26, 1920, the 19th Amendment to the U.S. Constitution is ratified which gave women the right to vote.

A study in Chicago from September 1965 to March 1966 showed that 46.1 percent of the major crimes committed against women took place in their own homes.

1967, one of the first U.S. battered women's shelters opens in Maine.

1970, a study in Oakland, California, showed that police responded to over 16,000 family disturbance calls in a six month period.

So, without debating whether or not a "Rule of Thumb" was ever a law sanctioned by any government institution, we can say that there has never been a law passed saying that a wife could not beat her husband. Nothing in our legal past ever said that a wife could hit her husband with a cast iron skillet no larger than sixteen inches in diameter, or it is unlawful for a husband to be struck with a rolling pin any longer than eighteen inches in length.

And, when I tried to understand why my Uncle Walter believed the way he did, and as I tried to understand why Ben and Chad had the beliefs that they did, which were obviously passed down to them from their father and possibly their grandfather's beliefs, I happened upon an old article from a May 13, 1955 "Housekeeping Monthly" magazine. There is a picture of a husband dressed in a suit, he is just walking in the door from work. There is a small boy and girl all dressed up, no grass or mud stains on their knees and no jelly smeared on their faces. The wife looks like June Cleaver from the old show, "Leave It To Beaver," with a nice dress, an apron and high heels. The woman is greeting the man with a big smile as she is stirring something in a pan on the stove. The following in italics is how the article reads:

"The good wife's guide

- *Have dinner ready. Plan ahead, even the night before, to have a delicious meal ready, on time for his return. This is a way of letting him know that you have been thinking about him and are concerned about his needs. Most men are hungry when they come home and the prospect of a good meal (especially his favorite dish) is part of the warm welcome needed.*

- *Prepare yourself. Take 15 minutes to rest so you'll be refreshed when he arrives. Touch up your make-up, put a ribbon in your hair and be fresh-looking. He has just been with a lot of work-weary people.*

- *Be a little gay and a little more interesting for him. His boring day may need a lift and one of your duties is to provide it.*

- *Clear away the clutter. Make one last trip through the main part of the house just before your husband arrives.*

- *Gather up schoolbooks, toys, paper, etc. and then run a dustcloth over the tables.*

- *Over the cooler months of the year you should prepare and light a fire for him to unwind by. Your husband will feel he has reached a haven of rest and order, and it will give you a lift too. After all, catering for his comfort will provide you with immense personal satisfaction.*

- *Prepare the children. Take a few minutes to wash the children's hands and faces (if they are small), comb their hair and, if necessary, change their clothes. They are little treasures and he would like to see them playing the part. Minimize all noise. At the time of his arrival, eliminate all noise of the washer, dryer or vacuum. Try to encourage the children to be quiet.*

- *Be happy to see him.*

- *Greet him with a warm smile and show sincerity in your desire to please him.*

- *Listen to him. You may have a dozen important things to tell him, but the moment of his arrival is not the time. Let him talk first, remember, his topics of conversation are more important than yours.*

- *Make the evening his. Never complain if he comes home late or goes out to dinner, or other places of entertainment without you. Instead, try to understand his world of strain and pressure and his very real need to be at home and relax.*

- *Your goal: Try to make sure your home is a place of peace, order and tranquility where your husband can renew himself in body and spirit.*

- *Don't greet him with complaints and problems.*

- *Don't complain if he's late home for dinner or even stays out all night. Count this as minor compared to what he might have gone through that day.*

- *Make him comfortable. Have him lean back in a comfortable chair or have him lie down in the bedroom. Have a cool or warm drink ready for him.*

- *Arrange his pillow and offer to take his shoes. Speak in a low, soothing and pleasant voice.*

- *Don't ask him questions about his actions or question his judgment or integrity. Remember, he is the master of the house and as such will always exercise his will with fairness and truthfulness. You have no right to question him.*

- *A good wife knows her place."*

Well, that was as hard to type as it was for you to read, and thank God things have changed. But, after reading that, without granting any excuses to men today who still believe these things, this article at least sheds some light on how some people have defined men's and women's roles over the years. My uncle, Ben and Chad are all stuck in 1955. After reading this article, can you see why 46.1 percent of major crimes perpetrated against women took place in their own homes? Can you see why the Oakland Police Department responded to 16,000 family disturbance calls in a six month period? What was going on in the 1960s and 1970s? The women's movement and societal beliefs about the role of women were changing, and some men were digging their heels into the ground, not willing to get onto the bandwagon. And we are only talking about beliefs and perceptions that are only 52 years old.

And let's go back a little earlier. What was the original design that God set up? Look at Genesis chapter 1, verses 27 and 28 (KJV), "So

God created man in his own image, in the image of God he created him; male and female he created them. And God blessed them," (who them? Adam and Eve them), "and God said unto them," (who them? Adam and Eve them), "Be fruitful, and multiply, and replenish the earth, and subdue it: and have dominion over the fish of the sea, and over the fowl of the air, and over every living thing that moveth upon the earth." I do not read any hierarchy in that command of either Adam over Eve or Eve over Adam. I get that there was a togetherness, an equality of purpose and direction. Adam still a protector and provider, Eve supplying strength and help as God had intended, and a harmonious, ruling over, multiplying and subduing together in a unity of purpose.

But God did predict that there would be this struggle between men and women. Not that God caused the situation, but that because of their fall from the Garden of Eden there were certain curses that came along with the sin that Adam and Eve committed with the serpent. The oneness, the lack of discord all came to an end when sin came into the picture. Because Adam was created first, there was some headship there, but it was not control and domination, it was the role of protector. I'm sure you have all seen the drawings of a cave man, with a club in one hand, dragging a woman by the hair into a cave, and this isn't at all what the picture of Adam and Eve was like in God's design. So Adam the protector, Eve the strong helper and companion to be with Adam.

So in Genesis 3 verses 5 and 6 we read of this conversation between the serpent and Eve, "For God knows that when you eat of it your eyes will be opened, and you will be like God, knowing good and evil," (NIV). "When the woman saw the fruit of the tree was good for food and pleasing to the eye, and also desirable for gaining wisdom, she took some and ate it. She also gave some to her husband, who was with her, and he ate it," (NIV). Then in verse 13 God asks Eve, "What is this that thou hast done?" And the woman said, "The serpent beguiled" (deceived) "me, and I did eat it," (KJV). And Adam, in the verse prior to that tried to pin the whole blame on Eve when he said to God, "The woman thou gavest to be with me, she gave me of the tree, and I did eat it," (KJV).

God then told Eve, in verse 16, "I will greatly multiply thy sorrow and thy conception; in sorrow thou shalt bring forth children; and thy desire shall be to thy husband, and he shall rule over you," (KJV). And the same verse in the NIV reads, "I will greatly increase your pain in childbearing; with pain you will give birth to children. Your desire will be for your husband, and he will rule over you."

In verse 17, God says to Adam, "Because you listened to your wife and ate from the tree about which I commanded you, 'You must not eat of it,' cursed is the ground because of you; through painful toil you will eat of it all the days of your life." God continues in verses 18 and 19, "It will produce thorns and thistles for you, and you will eat the plants of the field. By the sweat of your brow you will eat your food until you return to the ground..."

So when Eve listened to the serpent, in God's view, she had reversed the role as she should have turned to Adam for protection from the danger. By acting on her own and going against God's command, she sinned. And Adam sinned as he acted right along with Eve and even minimized his involvement and not only blamed Eve, but in a way blamed God by saying, "The woman YOU put here with me she gave me some fruit..."

So to Adam, he would no longer just be able to walk around and eat what God produced for him, he would have to sweat, toil and work hard to exist in life.

It's an interesting statement in verse 16 when God tells Eve, "...your desire will be for your husband and he will rule over you." Now, some guys have read this and said, "Gee, that's great, my wife won't be able to keep her hands off of me because even God said here that her desire will be for her husband." This is a great misunderstanding of the text. What God was saying is that while he originally designed this harmony and unity between them, that now, after sin had come into the world, things would change. Not by God's design, but a natural consequence of sin. If this desire that the wife would have over the husband was some sexual desire, and it meant that every day after Adam was out toiling in the field he would come home and Eve wouldn't be able to keep her hands off of him, it wouldn't be a curse. And people who are married know that wives just don't run around every day trying to be close and affectionate with their husbands just because he is out sweating and toiling and bringing home something to eat. The way to understand the verse is to look at the last part that reads, "he shall rule over thee."

The curse was a new way of life, not the great oneness that they had been used to before the serpent came along. Man's authority became corrupt, unreasonable, like that of a tyrant. God predicted that there would be male chauvinism and there has always been since the fall, this practice of man keeping a woman down. But we can see the original blueprint of God's design, that this was not what God had in mind when he created them in His image. And God just didn't throw them out of the garden and not show love and concern for them. We read in the same chapter, verse 21, "Unto Adam also and to his wife did the Lord God make coats of skins, and clothed them," (KJV). Did God create lies? No, that came as a result of sin. Did God create stealing? No, that, too, came from sin. Did God create male chauvinism? No, that, too, came from sin and it has been around since Adam and Eve.

The unbalanced result of sin is also shown when God said in verse 16 to Eve, "Your desire will be for your husband." This isn't a sexual desire because men usually have way stronger sexual desires than women do, so God can't be talking about a physical desire for intimacy. In Arabic this means to seek control. So, because of sin, the woman is trying to run things and the man is trying to keep her down, and not because God ordered that, it is a natural result from what happened in the Garden of Eden. And isn't that what sin seeks to do? It seeks to control us, and even the Apostle Paul tells us in 1Peter 5:8 and 9, "Be self-controlled and alert. Your enemy the devil prowls around like a roaring lion looking for someone to devour. Resist him, standing firm in the faith..."

There is this idea that a Christian will recognize that these controlling tendencies and these desires to keep our partner down are sinful desires and that we will stand firm and resist this sin. And so we see that this idea of domination has very deep roots in history. Even in Jesus' day women were looked down upon, they were viewed as something less than that of a man, they were looked at lower than even animals. And before you think that God had anything to do with that, look at how Jesus responded to woman. When Jesus went to talk to the woman at the well, there were two very astonishing things that happened there. The first was that a Jew would actually walk through Samaria. Jews hated the Samaritans and would walk great distances, going out of their way to not cut through that country while traveling. The second was that a Rabi would even consider talking to a woman, and a Samaritan woman at that. When the crowds were ready to stone a woman for accusations of adultery, who stepped up and faced the crowd and told them, anyone without sin cast the first stone? Jesus was there, defending a woman.

Who did ministry work with Jesus? Mary and Martha. Jesus didn't look down on them. Jesus recognized their spiritual gifts and afforded them opportunities to serve and be partners in spreading the gospel. When Jesus emerged from the tomb on resurrection day, whom did he choose to go tell the disciples the great news? He chose Mary Magdalene, Joanna, and Mary the mother of James, and when they went to the eleven apostles and told them what the angels had said, we read in Luke 24:11, "But they did not believe the women, because their words seemed like nonsense." And not to mention that in those days a woman's word or testimony meant nothing, it was not believed.

So, I hope that we all have a better understanding of the roots of control and domination, and I hope that we understand what God's viewpoint is – that God was not the one who ever designed or developed chauvinism.

Chapter Four

How Should The Church Respond to Abuse?

TIFFANY WALKS UP TO HER Priest after Mass and says, "Father, can I ask you something? I just don't know what to do. Herman is so rough with me, he screams and yells at me, he slaps me, he pushes me. I haven't told anyone and I'm coming to you for guidance and advice." Her Priest tells her, "Your job is to be a good mother and a good wife. Go back and obey, do what is pleasing to the Lord."

Ethel goes to the church ladies Mug and Muffin mid-week, morning Bible study. During prayer request time, Ethel breaks down and cries and pleads with the women, "Please pray for me, I'm considering a divorce from George. I've never told anyone here, but I've been coming here for some time now and I feel safe to share this with all of you. George chased me around the dining room table with his shoe in his hand last night. After he caught me, he beat my back and head with it and this isn't the first time. This has been going on for years and I just can't take it anymore." Barb looks as astonished as the other women and responds, "A divorce? You can't get a divorce, don't you know that's the unpardonable sin?"

Gigi stops in at church Tuesday morning because Pastor's car is there. She is hoping to approach him alone and tell her of her problems at home. The church secretary leads her to the Pastor's study and she sits down in a chair. Gigi's knees are knocking together as she cries and struggles to blurt out the problem. She finally tells him, "Steve is terrible to me and the kids. He has beaten us for years and it's getting worse. I don't feel safe and the kids aren't safe either. What should I do?" The pastor takes his glasses off and sets them on his desk and says, "Remember Gigi, you stood right here in this church, at the alter, and in front of your family, friends, the congregation and even God you took an oath, an oath to stay with Steve, 'for better or for worse.'"

I am currently involved with a new church plant where I live and serve on the advisory team. Before that, I served four years as an elder of a non-denominational Christian church. I can tell you that there are many hurt people and hurting marriages within the walls of churches everywhere. I was a volunteer in the youth ministries area and ran many middle school and high school Sunday school classes and mid-week Bible studies. So, many troubled teens would come to me and confide in me that their home lives were a wreck, that domestic violence was so bad, they thought of running away, or some had suicidal thoughts because they just couldn't take the day-to-day strain any longer.

When someone at church discloses that they are a victim of domestic violence, they are usually told to go home and be obedient. They are told, "Go read Romans 8:28, 'And we know that in all things God works for the good of those who love him, who have been called according to his purpose.'" So, is a victim of violence supposed to read this and think, "Gee, I must not love God enough because then this wouldn't be happening to me?" Or, should the response be, "Oh, well, I guess there is nothing that can be done, it's all going to work itself out for good some day." Absolutely not! While I believe that God does work, in all things, for the good of those who love him, this verse does very little to bring comfort to the victim, nor does it bring about a change in the situation of the abused.

I think that many pastors, priests, elders and deacons lack the understanding of abuse, they do not understand what abuse does to people, they do not know how to intervene (in a meaningful way) into the abusive situation, they do not know how to confront the abuser, they do not want to confront the abuser – especially when the abuser is also a member of the congregation. Or, worse yet, the abuser is an elder, Sunday school teacher or even pastor at the church. I don't believe that these church leaders do not care. I think that there has never been training and teaching in this area. And the good news is that I hope to bring about a better understanding of what the role of the church and especially what the role of church leaders should be when confronted by such a delicate, yet very important intervention.

What does not help is to simply tell the abused person, "Well, hang in there, we'll be praying for you." Not that prayer does not help. Not that prayer does not change things, but look at what James told us in chapter 2, verses 14 through 17, "What good is it, my brothers, if a man claims to have faith but has no deeds? Can such faith save him? Suppose a brother or sister is without clothes and daily food. If one of you says to him, 'Go, I wish you well; keep warm and well fed,' but does nothing about his physical needs, what good is it? In the same way, faith by itself, if it is not accompanied by action is dead," (NIV). Or, in the King James Version: "What doth it profit, my brethren, though a man say he hath faith, and have not works? Can faith save him? If a brother or sister be naked, and destitute of daily food, and one of you say unto them, 'Depart in peace, be ye warmed and filled;' notwithstanding ye give them not those things which are needful to the body; what doth it profit? Even so faith, if it hath not works, is dead, being alone." And my all-time favorite translation of this comes from Eugene Peterson's "The Message" contemporary translation which reads: "Dear friends, do you think you'll get anywhere in this if you learn all the right words but never do anything? Does merely talking about faith indicate that a person really has it? For instance, you come upon an old friend dressed in rags and half-starved and say, 'Good morning friend! Be clothed in Christ! Be filled with the Holy Spirit!' And walk off without providing so much as a coat or a cup of soup – where does that get you? Isn't it obvious that God-talk without God-acts is outrageous nonsense?"

And when a victim of violence comes to a fellow believer and we do nothing to help them, we not only leave them hanging there with no help, we expose them to continued, escalating violence and somehow convince them that the situation that they are in must be God's will.

Kathy finally drove to her mom and dad's house. It was odd that her mom would not answer the phone all day. Dad goes out golfing sometimes with his retirees group, but he didn't even answer his cell phone. Kathy just had to stop by the house and make sure that they were O.K. Kathy knocked and she rang the doorbell. She looked in the windows of the garage and both cars were there. "This is odd," Kathy said to herself as she went back to her car to get the keys that she has to her parents' house. Kathy opened the door and let out a loud scream, and then cries for help as she saw her mom laying lifeless on the big oval rug in the living room. Kathy dialed 9-1-1 and told them to send an ambulance. "She isn't breathing! She has no pulse. Come quickly!" The 9-1-1 operator stayed on the line with Kathy to instruct her on how to perform CPR, and in the back of Kathy's mind she is wondering where her dad is, is he injured or dead, too? The paramedics and the police arrive. The paramedics have her mom hooked up to a heart monitor, they have taken over CPR and are starting an IV. Kathy is talking to the police, and the officers start looking around the house for Kathy's dad. The paramedics stop their work and they tell Kathy that there is nothing that they can do. They explain that they estimate that her mom died several hours ago. Kathy buries her face into her hands and sobs uncontrollably and says, "No, no, this can't be happening!"

Kathy calls her husband who is equally shocked and on his way. The police ask Kathy to sit down in the kitchen and she does. The one officer tells her, "Ma'am, I am so sorry, but we have some more bad news." Kathy knows that it's her dad, he must be injured, or worse yet, dead, too. The officer tells her, "Your father, he is in the basement." Kathy jumps up to go to the stairs. The police stop her, "Please, Kathy, don't go down there!" the officer pleads. He then tells her that her dad is also dead, that he hung himself with a rope and there is nothing that anyone can do for him either. Kathy sobs and sobs and blurts out, "Were they murdered? Who could have done this?" The officer tells her that there is a note on the dryer right next to him. They tell her that it appears her father wrote it. The note is an apology to Kathy and her brother, that her dad said he and mom were arguing and he "just lost it," and strangled Lois. After he saw what he had done, he wrote that he just couldn't go on and decided to take his own life.

Kathy thinks back to her childhood years, growing up here, and she remembers the arguing, the outbursts, she remembers the bruises – the bruises on her mom's arms and legs. She knew that her mom was abused, but her mom didn't say much about it. Kathy thought that it had all ended, it was something that no one talked much about. At the funeral, Mrs. Winters who lives next door to Kathy's parents walks up to Kathy and they both hug and cry. "I should have done something, I should have said something, I feel so responsible," Mrs. Winters says. "What do you mean?" Kathy asks between sobs. "They yelled a lot, I would hear your mom yell for him to stop hitting her." "When was the last time you heard them?" Kathy wondered. "Well, it was all of the time, but the last time was just yesterday. I tried to ask your mom about it, but it's just one of those things . . . well you know, that's so hard to talk about."

Trudy and Cal had the most beautiful outside wedding just three months ago in July. The weather was perfect. All of their family and friends were there. Cal was the perfect soul mate and, best of all, he really loved Trudy's two and a half year old son Reilly. Other men Trudy had dated really didn't want "an instant family," they would tell her. But not Cal. He was very helpful to Trudy, and Reilly was even calling him "Daddy" now. Trudy met Cal at work, in a small factory just outside of town. They worked the same shift and just two departments away from each other.

So, on that nice, warm October day, Trudy's immediate supervisor went to Cal's supervisor and asked, "Where is Cal? You'd think that if Trudy was sick today, she would at least call in, or one would think that Cal would have stopped over at my desk and say something." Cal's boss said, "Well, I have to tell you, I thought Cal was sick today and I was just coming over to check in with Trudy." So, they check the employee roster and call the home. "Nope, just the answering machine." They try both cell phones, no answer. "Well, perhaps they are running late, let's give them a bit." When that bit turned into three more hours, one supervisor said, "Well, maybe they had car trouble or something. I'll swing over there to the house. I have to pick up some stuff from the print shop anyway."

The boss pulls into the driveway, "That's odd, both of their cars are still here." He walks up to the front porch and hears little Reilly crying. "Ahh, the baby is sick today, but they should have called," he says to himself and rings the doorbell. Well, there is no answer, so he knocks and he rings the bell repeatedly. Nothing from inside. He can see Reilly, standing in the hallway, just wearing a diaper and a t-shirt and crying. The boss goes to the back door and knocks and knocks, no answer, just Reilly walking around and crying. He drags a picnic table over to the back window of the kitchen, climbs up and looks in. His stomach turns inside out as he sees Trudy laying on the floor in a pool of blood. He dials 9-1-1, the police are on their way, and he takes a brick from the fire pit and breaks the window in the door and cautiously walks in. Reilly runs away crying, he is calling out in a shaking voice, "Trudy! Are you O.K.? Cal! Where are you?!"

The police arrive and give Reilly to him and ask him to take the child outside. By this time he has had a chance to call back to the office and the other supervisor is stunned, "You have got to be kidding me," she says. The medical examiner estimates that Trudy died about six hours ago. Three rounds from Cal's 9mm handgun. Cal is in the den. Cal has a single, self-inflicted gunshot wound to the head. Reilly is just lucky to be alive and will need lots of counseling – not just because he lost his mom, but because of the gruesome scene that he was exposed to for many hours. Trudy's family and friends and co-workers are stunned. They hold a candlelight vigil for her outside of the home that night. They sing some songs and recall happy memories, but mainly they look at each other, they look at that house, and not one there had any idea that Trudy and Cal had any problems. Trudy's parents hear Reilly say later, "Daddy hit mommy. Daddy push mommy down stairs." Trudy's mom just can't understand what happened, and she doesn't understand why Trudy wouldn't have come to her sooner if there was a problem.

These are true stories. I tried to spare you too many grizzly details, and I wanted you to see just how awful domestic violence can become. Neighbors are aware of violence in a home, just like Mrs. Winters, but they seldom times call the police. Family members and co-workers may suspect something, but oftentimes they never approach the topic with the victim. You may know someone in your office at work who has an occasional bruise, but you say nothing. This same person may receive 20 phone calls in a two hour period from their abusing spouse. You see the frustration on her face, you see the tear in her eye, you hear her whispering on the phone, you hear her telling the caller, "Please quit calling, I'm going to get fired," but you say nothing. These are little hints that we can all pick up on.

In Cal and Trudy's case, though, no one knew anything. No one would have suspected anything. Cal and Trudy took all of their breaks together, they ate lunch together and not one person who worked with them would have ever dreamed that Trudy was living in a nightmare of verbal, emotional and physical abuse. To the abuser, domestic violence at home is their "little secret," they do not want anyone else to know. I have never known an abuser to go to work the next day and at the coffee pot announce to others, "Hey, I slapped my wife last night," or, "I punched my husband in the nose last night." In fact, in most cases where an abuser does get found out, they usually sell the house and move to a new neighborhood or they find a new job. An abuser knows that what they are doing at home is wrong and they will do anything to hide this from others.

The victim, in most cases, will never disclose that they are being abused because of embarrassment, or they try to convince themselves, "He will never do that again, he told me he won't." Victims are threatened to keep quiet. The abuser will tell them that if they ever "breathe one word of this to anyone," that next time the beating will be worse, or "I'll take the kids and you'll never find me," or, "I'll kill you." A victim who has been abused by an intimate partner has every right to believe that the abuser will make good on these threats. That is why when law enforcement, or anyone first becomes aware that a person is being victimized at home, some intervention needs to take place. If nothing changes, nothing changes and the abuse escalates.

When you are reading the paper or watching the news, try to see just how many headlines there are that deal with domestic violence. Here's a sampling, and there are many more and they are more and more frequent:

"Newlyweds in murder-suicide," "Man arrested after ramming ex-wife's car," "Man admits lighting fire that killed his girlfriend," "Man in custody after subjecting his wife to several days of physical abuse," "Police: Man threatens to kill girlfriend," "Man kills wife, their three children, self," "Woman faces charge of battering boyfriend," "Police officer kills pregnant girlfriend – bond set at $5 million," "Chicago area man allegedly killed his wife, two children," "Body found believed to be missing wife – police suspect husband," "Man faces charges in baby's death – infant shook after argument with wife," "Abuse survivor forms foster agency for pets – her abusing husband killed her cats," "Family begs others to report violence after death of their adult daughter," "911 tape indicates man shot ex, others," "Loved ones seek solace at vigil." The day after the West Virginia shooting rampage, buried on page five in a one column three inch article I read, "Father kills children, self to retaliate against wife," "Pro wrestler kills wife, children, self, steroid use suspected, roid-rage or anger?"

Here are some statistics that show us just how dangerous domestic violence can be for victims and their children:

This information comes from the Centers for Disease Control and Prevention, www.cdc.gov. Their Intimate Partner Violence statistics come from police agencies, clinical settings, nongovernmental organizations and survey research. The CDC finds, "Most Intimate Partner Violence incidents are not reported to police. About 20 percent of IPV rapes or sexual assault, 25 percent of physical assaults, and 50 percent of stalkings directed toward women are reported." Even fewer IPV incidents against men are reported (Tjaden and Thoennes 2000a). Thus, it is believed that available data greatly underestimate the true magnitude of the problem. While not an exhaustive list, here are some statistics on the occurrence of IPV. In many cases, the severity of the IPV behaviors is unknown.

Nearly 5.3 million incidents of IPV occur each year among U.S. women ages 18 and older, and 3.2 million occur among men. Most assaults are relatively minor and consist of pushing, grabbing, shoving, slapping and hitting (Tjaden and Thoennes 2000a).

In the United States every year, about 1.5 million women and more than 800,000 men are raped or physically assaulted by an intimate partner. This translates into about 47 IPV assaults per 1,000 women and 32 assaults per 1,000 men (Tjaden and Thoennes 2000a).

IPV results in nearly 2 million injuries and 1,300 deaths nationwide every year (CDC 2003).

Estimates indicate more than 1 million women and 371,000 men are stalked by intimate partners each year (Tjaden and Thoennes 2000a).

IPV accounted for 20 percent of nonfatal violence against women in 2001 and 3 percent against men (Rennison 2003).

From 1976 to 2002, about 11 percent of homicide victims were killed by an intimate partner (Fox and Zawitz 2004).

In 2002, 76 percent of IPV homicide victims were female; 24 percent were male (Fox and Zawitz 2004).

The number of intimate partner homicides decreased 14 percent overall for men and women in the span of about 20 years, with a 67 percent decrease for men (from 1,357 to 388) vs. 25 percent for women (1,600 to 1,202) (Fox and Zawitz 2004).

One study found that 44 percent of women murdered by their intimate partner had visited an emergency department within two years of the homicide.

Previous literature suggests that women who have separated from their abuse partners often remain at risk of violence (Campbell, et al. 2003; Fleury, Sullivan and Bybee 2000).

Firearms were the major weapon type used in intimate partner homicides from 1981 to 1989 (Paulozzi, et al. 2001).

A national study found that 29 percent of women and 22 percent of men had experienced physical, sexual or psychological IPV during their lifetime (Coker, et al. 2002).

Between 4 percent and 8 percent of pregnant women are abused at least once during their pregnancy (Gazmararian, et al. 2000).

In general, victims of repeated violence over time experience more serious consequences than victims of one-time incidents (Johnson and Leone 2005).

At least 42 percent of women and 20 percent of men who were physically assaulted since age 18 sustained injuries during their most recent victimization. Most injuries were minor such as scratches, bruises and welts (Tjaden and Thoennes 2000a).

More severe physical consequences of IPV may occur depending on severity and frequency of abuse (Campbell, et al. 2002; Heise and Garcia-Moreno 2002; Plichta 2004; Tjaden and Thoennes 2000a).

These include:

- Bruises

- Knife wounds

- Pelvic pain

- Headaches

- Back pain

- Broken bones

- Gynecological disorders

- Pregnancy difficulties like low birth weight babies and perinatal deaths

- Sexually transmitted diseases including HIV/AIDS

- Central nervous system disorders

- Gastrointestinal disorders

- Symptoms of post-traumatic stress disorder (emotional detachment, sleep disturbances, flashbacks, replaying assault in mind)

- Heart or circulatory conditions.

Children may become injured during IPV incidents between their parents. A large overlap exists between IPV and child maltreatment

(Appel and Holden 1998). One study found that children of abused mothers were 57 times more likely to have been harmed because of IPV between their parents, compared with children of non-abused mothers (Parkinson, et al. 2001).

Physical violence is typically accompanied by emotional or psychological abuse (Tjaden and Thoennes 2000a). IPV – whether sexual, physical or psychological – can lead to various psychological consequences for victims (Bergen 1996; Coker, et al. 2002; Heise and Garcia-Moreno 2002; Roberts, Klein and Fisher 2003):

- Depression

- Antisocial behavior

- Suicidal behavior in females

- Anxiety

- Low self-esteem

- Inability to trust men

- Fear of intimacy

Victims of IPV sometimes face the following social consequences (Heise and Garcia-Moreno 2002; Pichta 2004):

- Restricted access to services

- Strained relationships with health providers and employers

- Isolation from social networks

Women with a history of IPV are more likely to display behaviors that present further health risks (e.g., substance abuse, alcoholism, suicide attempts).

IPV is associated with a variety of negative health behaviors (Heise and Garcia-Moreno 2002; Plichta 2004; Roberts, Auinger and Klein 2005; Silverman, et al. 2001). Studies show that the more severe the violence, the stronger its relationship to negative health behaviors by victims.

- Engaging in high-risk sexual behavior – unprotected sex, decreased condom use, early sexual initiation, choosing unhealthy sexual partners, having multiple sex partners, trading sex for food, money or other items.

- Using or abusing harmful substances - smoking cigarettes, drinking alcohol, driving after drinking alcohol, taking drugs.

- Unhealthy diet-related behaviors - fasting, vomiting, abusing diet pills, overeating.

- Overuse of health services.

Economic impact of IPV:

- Costs of IPV against women in 1995 exceed an estimated $5.8 billion. These costs include nearly $4.1 billion in the direct costs of medical and mental health care and nearly $1.8 billion in the indirect costs of lost productivity (CDC 2003).

- When updated to 2003 dollars, IPV costs exceed $8.3 billion, which includes $460 million for rape, $6.2 billion for physical assault, $461 million for stalking and $1.2 billion in the value of lost lives (Max, et al. 2004).

- Victims of severe IPV lose nearly 8 million days of paid work – the equivalent of more than 32,000 full-time jobs – and almost 5.6 million days of household productivity each year (CDC 2003).

- Women who experience severe aggression by men (e.g., not being allowed to go to work or school or having their lives or their children's lives threatened) are more likely to have been unemployed in the past, have health problems, and be receiving public assistance (Lloyd and Taluc 1999).

References

Appel, A.E., Holden, G.W. The co-occurrence of spouse and physical child abuse: a review and appraisal. Journal of Family Psychology 1998; 12:578-99.

Archer, J. Sex differences in aggression between heterosexual partners: a meta-analytic review. Psychological Bulletin 2000; 126(5):651-80.

Bergen, R.K. Wife rape; understanding the response of survivors and service providers. Thousand Oaks (CA: Sage; 1996).

Black, D.A., Schumacher, J.A., Smith, A.M., Heyman, R.E. Partner, child abuse risk factor literature review: National Network on Family Resiliency, National Network for Health; 1999 [cited 2005 September 15]. Available from URL: www.nnh.org/risk.

Blum, R.W,, Ireland, M. Reducing risk, increasing protective factors: Findings from the Caribbean Youth Health Survey. Journal of Adolescent Health 2004; 35(6):493-500.

Campbell, J.C., Webster, D., Koziol-McLain, J., Block, C., Campbell, D., Curry, M.A., et al. Risk factors for femicide in abusive relationships: results from a multisite case control study. American Journal of Public Health 2003;93:1089-97.

Campbell, J.C., Jones, A.S., Dienemann, J., Kub, J., Schollenberger, J., O'Campo, P., et al. Intimate partner violence and physical health consequences. Archives of Internal Medicine 2002;162(10):1157-63.

Centers for Disease Control and Prevention (CDC). Costs of intimate partner violence against women in the United States. Atlanta (GA): CDC, National Center for Injury Prevention and Control; 2003. [cited 2005 September 15]. Available from: URL: www.cdc.gov/ncipc/pub-res/ipv_cost/ipv.htm.

Coker, A.L., Smith, P.H., Thompson, M.P., McKeown, R.E., Bethea, L., David, K.E. Social support projects against negative effects of partner violence on mental health. Journal of Women's Health and Gender-Based Medicine 2002;11(5):465-76.

Crandall, M., Nathens, A.B., Kernic, M.A., Holt, V.L., Rivera, F.P. Predicting future injury among women in abusive relationships. Journal of Trauma-Injury Infection and Critical Care 2004;2004;56(4):96-12.

Fleury, R.E., Sullivan, C.M., Bybee, D.I. When ending the relationship does not end the violence. Women's experiences of violence by former partners. Violence Against Women 2000;6:1363-83.

Fox, J.A., Zawitz, M.W. Homicide trends in the United States. Washington (DC): Department of Justice (US); 2004. [cited 2005 September 15]. Available from: URL: www.ojp.usdoj.gov/bjs/homicide/hotrnd.htm.

Gazmarian, J.A., Petersen, R., Spitz, A.M., Goodwin, M.M., Saltzman, L.E., Marks, J.S. Violence and reproductive health: current knowledge and future research directions. Maternal and Child Health Journal 2000;4(2):79-84.

Heise, L., Garcia-Moreno, C. Violence by intimate partners. In: Krug E, Dahlberg LL, Mercy JA, et al., editors. World report on violence and health. Geneva (Switzerland): World Health organization; 2002.p. 87-121.

Johnson, M.P., Leone, J.M. The differential effects of intimate terrorism and situational couple violence. Journal of Family Issues 26(3):322-49.

Kantor, G.K., Jalenski, J.L. Dynamics and risk factors in partner violence. In: Jasinski JL, Williams LM, editors. Partner violence: a comprehensive review of 20 years of research. Thousand Oaks (CA): Sage, 1998. p. 1-43.

Lloyd, S., Taluc, N. The effects of male violence on female employment. Violence Against Women 1999; 5:370-92.

Max, W., Rice, D.P., Finkenstein, E., Bardwell, R.A., Leadbetter, S. The economic toll of intimate partner violence against women in the United States. Violence and Victims 2004;19(3):259-72.

Parkinson, G.W., Adams, R.C., Emerling, F.G. Maternal domestic violence screening in an office-based pediatric practice. Pediatrics 2001:108(3):E43.

Paulozzi, L.J., Saltzman, L.A., Thompson, M.J., Holmgren, P. Surveillance for homicide among intimate partners – United States, 1981-1998. CDC Surveillance Summaries 2001;50(SS-3):1-16.

Plichta, S.B. Intimate partner violence and physical health consequences: policy and practice implications. Journal of Interpersonal Violence 2004; 19(11):1296-323.

Rennison, C. Intimate partner violence, 1993-2001. Washington (DC): Bureau of Justice Statistics, Department of Justice (US);2003. Public No. NCJ197838.

Roberts, T.A., Auinger, P., Klein, J.D. Intimate partner abuse and the reproductive health of sexually active female adolescents. Journal of Adolescent Health 2005;36(5):380-5.

Roberts, T.A., Klein, J.D., Fisher, S. Longitude effect of intimate partner abuse on high-risk behavior among adolescents. Archives of Pediatrics and Adolescent Medicine 2003; 157(9):875-81.

Saltzman, L.E., Fanslow, J.L., McMahon, P.M., Shelly, G.A. Intimate partner violence: uniform definitions and recommended data elements. Atlanta (GA): Centers for Disease Control and Prevention, National Center for Injury Prevention and Control; 2002.

Silverman, J.G., Raj, A., Mucci, L., Hathaway, J. Dating violence against adolescent girls and associated substance use, unhealthy weight control, sexual risk behavior, pregnancy, and suicidality. Journal of the American Medical Association 2001;285(5):572-9.

Tjaden, P., Thoennes, N. Extent, nature and consequences of intimate partner violence: findings from the National Violence Against Women Survey. Washington (DC): Department of Justice (US); 200a. Publication No. NCJ 181867. [cited 2005 September 15]. Available from URL: www.ojp.usdoj.gov/nij/pubs-sum/181867.htm.

Tjaden, P., Thoennes, N. Full report of the prevalence, incidence and consequences of violence against women: findings from the National Violence Against Women Survey. Washington (DC): Department of Justice (US); 2000b. Publication No. NCJ 183781. [cited 2005 September 15]. Available from URL: www.ncjrs.org/txtfiles1/nij/183781.txt.

I purposely placed these references here, in this chapter, rather than burying them in an appendix so that you can see where those statistics come from. I have cited these numbers to people before who have shrugged them off as just data collected from domestic violence agencies. Now, here are some statistics from actual advocacy agencies, which are very accurate and, interestingly, support the findings of the previously listed studies.

According to the Wisconsin Coalition Against Domestic Violence (WCADV):

- In 2000, 25,021 incidents of domestic abuse were reported to the Wisconsin Department of Justice. (Domestic Abuse Incident Report for 2000, Office of Victim Services.)

- Shelters provided 132,652 nights of shelter in 2000, 104,998 in 1999 and 101,558 in 1998. (Department of Health and Family Services, Domestic Abuse Program, 2002.)

- In 2000, there were 61,124 hotline calls received. (DHFS, Domestic Abuse Program, 2002.)

- A total of 3,853 cases of suspected abuse and neglect were reported in 2003. This represents an increase of 3.6 percent in reported cases since 2002. Sixteen cases were fatal and 357 were life threatening. Over 1 in 11 (9.3 percent) involved either a fatal or life-threatening situation. (Wisconsin DHFS, Division of Disability and Elder Services, Bureau of Aging and Long Term Care Resources, 2003.)

- 49 people were killed in Wisconsin domestic homicides in 2002. Thirty-eight were murdered and 11 perpetrators committed suicide. (WCADV 2002 Domestic Homicide Report.)

In the United States:

- Approximately 1.5 million women are physically assaulted by an intimate partner in the United States. (National Institute of Justice & Centers for Disease Control, National Violence Against Women Survey, 1998.)

- Approximately 90 to 95 percent of domestic violence victims are women. (Bureau of Justice Statistics Selected Findings, 1994.)

- A woman is more likely to be assaulted, injured, raped or killed by a male partner than by any other type of assailant. (Bureau of Justice Statistics, National Crime Victimization Study, 1995.)

- Women are more often victims of domestic violence than victims of burglary, mugging or other physical crimes combined. ("First Comprehensive National Survey of American Women," Commonwealth July 1993.)

- Among victims of violence committed by an intimate, the victimization rate of women, separated from their husbands was about three times higher than that of divorced women and about 25 times higher than that of married women. (Bureau of Justice Statistics, National Crime Victimization Study, 1995.) (Author's note: People trying to intervene in a domestic abuse situation often tell the victim to seek shelter at a domestic abuse shelter or offer to let the victim live with them for a while until the abuser and the victim can "reconcile." These are the most dangerous times for victims, and most victims who are killed by their abuser have died after receiving a restraining order or while packing some things to move out.)

- One-third to one-half of homeless women are on the street because they are fleeing domestic violence. (U.S. Department of Justice, February 1992.)

- It is often more dangerous for battered women after they leave a violent relationship. Although divorced and separated women compose only ten percent of all women in this situation, they account for 75 percent of all battered women. Divorced and separated women reported being physically abused fourteen times as often as women still living with their partners. (Raphael, Jody, Saving Bernice: Battered Women, Welfare and Poverty, 2000.)

- Divorced or separated persons had the highest rate of violence committed by relatives. (Bureau of Justice Statistics, "Criminal

Victimization in the United States, 1990," Washington D.C.: U.S. Department of Justice, February 1992.)

- Three million children in the United States are exposed to domestic violence in their homes each year. (American Psychology Association, Violence in the Family: Report of the American Psychological Association Presidential Task Force on Violence in the Family.)

What effect does domestic violence have on victims at work? I found this article on Yahoo! News by Ellen Wulfhorst on August 19, 2007:

"DOMESTIC VIOLENCE TAKES TOLL IN WORKPLACE

Victims of domestic violence suffer at work as well as home, losing costly work hours to distraction and absenteeism, new research shows. Women who were victims in the last year lost an average of 249 work hours to distraction, some 40 percent more than non-victims, according to research presented this week to the Academy of Management.

'In many cases, getting the attention and involvement of for-profit business organizations will require a demonstration of the bottom line costs they incur,' said the study by Carol Reeves, Collette Arens Bates and Anne O'Leary-Kelly of the University of Arkansas. 'This provides that type of evidence,' it said. 'Employers do not have to choose between minimizing their operating costs and "doing the right thing."

So-called intimate partner violence costs nearly $1.8 billion in lost productivity a year, with nearly 8 million paid workdays lost, according to the Centers for Disease Control and Prevention, National Center for Injury Prevention and Control. Overall, about 40 percent of women and 29 percent of men reported violence from intimate partners at some point in their lives, said the study of almost 2,400 U.S. workers.

'Any time you have 40 percent of your work force dealing with something, I think that requires attention because that number is huge,' Reeves said. Ten percent said the violence took place in the past year and were most likely to suffer in job performance.

Distractions included difficulty concentrating, working slowly, having to do work over or doing no work at all. Male victims lost 244 hours a year to distraction, compared with 202 hours for non-victims, it said. Women who suffered recent violence also missed 143 hours of work to tardiness or absenteeism, some 26 percent more than non-victims, it said.

In an effort to determine how many U.S. companies have programs to deal with the issue, a survey last year by the Corporate Alliance to End Partner Violence found about a third of workers believed their company had such a program.

An anti-violence program at Liz Claiborne Inc. has handled over 80 cases in the last five years, although many of its 8,000 U.S. employees may have used its referral services without alerting the firm, spokeswoman Jane Randel said. 'People look for the black eye, but it's not always going to be that,' she said. 'Things aren't always exactly what they seem.'

The program's assistance ranges from changing employees' telephone numbers to helping them relocate, she said. 'Our responsibility is to keep this person and those around her safe in the workplace,' Randel said.

Of the recent victims in the study, one in five reported the problem reaching to their workplace, mostly by stalking.

The researchers surveyed employees at an insurance company, a transportation company and an educational institution. Their findings were presented at the annual meeting of the Academy of Management, a research and teaching organization with nearly 17,000 members."

The American Institute on Domestic Violence also weighs in on the effects of domestic violence in the workplace. Their findings:

- The health-related costs of rape, physical assault, stalking and homicide by intimate partners exceed $5.8 billion each year.

- Of this total, nearly $4.1 billion is for victims requiring direct medical and mental health care services.

- Lost productivity and earnings due to intimate partner violence accounts for almost $1.8 billion each year.

- Intimate partner violence victims lose nearly 8 million days of paid work each year – the equivalent of more than 32,000 full-time jobs and nearly 5.6 million days of household productivity.

- 94 percent of corporate security directors rank domestic violence as a high security-risk.

- 78 percent of human resources directors identify domestic violence as a substantial employee problem.

- 56 percent of corporate leaders are personally aware of specific employees who are affected by domestic violence.

- 60 percent of senior executives said that domestic violence has a harmful effect on their company's productivity.

- 1,232 women are killed each year by an intimate partner.

- 5.3 million women are abused each year.

- Over 500,000 women are stalked by an intimate partner each year.

- Homicide is the leading cause of death for women in the workplace.

- Of the approximately 1.7 million incidents of workplace violence that occur in the U.S. every year, 18,700 are committed by an intimate partner; a current or former spouse, lover, partner or boyfriend/girlfriend.

- 96 percent of battered workers experience problems at work due to abuse.

- 74 percent of battered workers are harassed while at work by their abuser.

- 56 percent of battered workers are late to work, 28 percent leave work early, 54 percent miss entire days of work.

According to the National Coalition Against Domestic Violence, Psychological Abuse is defined as: *"...the systematic perpetration of malicious and explicit **nonphysical** acts against an intimate partner, child, or dependent adult.[1] This can include threatening the physical health of the victim and the victim's loved ones, controlling the victim's freedom, and effectively acting to destabilize or isolate the victim.[2] Psychological abuse frequently occurs prior to or concurrently with physical or sexual abuse.[3] While psychological abuse increases the trauma of physical and sexual abuse, a number of studies have demonstrated that psychological abuse independently causes long-term damage to its victim's mental health.* [1]Hamby, S.L. & Sugarman, D.B. (1999) Acts of Psychological Aggression Against a Partner and Their Relation to Physical Assault and Gender. Journal of Marriage and Family, 61(4), 959-970. [2]Follingstad, D.R. & DeHart, D.D. (2000). Defining Psychological Abuse of Husbands Towards Wives; Contexts, Behaviors, and Typologies. Journal of Interpersonal Violence, 15(9), 891-902. [3]Carlson, B.E., et al. (2002). Intimate Partner Abuse and Mental Health: The Role of Social Support and Other Protective Factors. Violence Against Women Journal, 8(6), 720-745.

Did you notice that the definition of Psychological Abuse includes the term – "nonphysical acts." So many abusers will tell you, "I've never laid one finger on her." That is because abusers who use psychological means do not need to lift one finger. Their power and control comes through threats to injure the victim, or threats to kill the victim's relatives or pets. Their power comes through damaging things that the victim cherishes, or keeping the victim from sleeping, eating or even leaving the house. The abuser refuses to let her talk to friends or relatives on the phone and may deny the victim any access to money. The victim will usually receive many phone calls from the abuser while she/he is at work. Co-workers will notice that the victim seems very embarrassed or under a great deal of stress while on the phone. Here are just a couple examples of psychological abuse.

It is Friday and everyone at work is happy for two reasons, they get a weekend off and it is payday. Sherri hates it. She hates it for two reasons. The weekend for her means two whole days stuck at home with her obnoxious and demanding husband. Payday also causes lots of stress for her because she knows that Raymond will be driving through the parking lot in about 30 minutes to pick up her paycheck, before she even gets out of work. Raymond does not work. He has never been able to hold down a job. Raymond will get fired after two weeks, just up and quit, or claim an injury and end up never going back. Sherri is the sole breadwinner, and works 50 hours a week, yet she never has any money, and bills that she really wants to pay never get paid. Raymond will park right in front of the break room, lay on the horn until Sherri comes out and she had better have her paycheck, already endorsed on the back, and she must hand it over to him. She told her pastor what is going on and she was told that she must just obey Raymond and that others will be praying for her. But all she sees is that Raymond is preying on her. She cannot concentrate on anything, she thinks of just taking a bottle of pills and ending it all. She abuses alcohol to escape the misery while at home, and she knows that her health is suffering as a result of what she deals with.

Agnes is 83 years old and lives in the same home that she and her husband built 51 years ago. She has been widowed now for 20 years, and her 49 year old son Peter lives with her. Peter has never left home, has never married and has never dated. Peter has no friends and delivers pizzas part time but only works about 12 hours a week. When he is home, she is never allowed to watch anything on T.V. that she wants to watch. She had several lady friends whom she used to play cards with, but Peter put a kibosh to that a long time ago. He told her that he could not stand sitting around listening to her and her friends talking and laughing for hours on end. When her friends do call, Peter tells them that his mom is sleeping or isn't feeling well. When her Social Security check comes, Peter demands that she sign it and he hurries off to the bank to cash it. He comes back home and gives her a small portion of her check and he pockets the rest.

Peter has never hit his mom, but he has broken several pieces of her fine china, and he threatens to break more if she questions him about anything or complains about her life. Agnes isn't allowed to leave the house. One day when Peter went to work, she stepped outside and struck up a conversation with a neighbor. Peter happened to drive past while making a delivery and he slammed on the brakes, stormed up to his mother, grabbed her arm and escorted her back into the house. "MOTHER! WHAT IS WRONG WITH YOU? HAVEN'T I TOLD YOU THAT YOU CANNOT LEAVE THE HOUSE!!" Peter delivered that pizza, called in sick for the rest of his shift, went to the hardware store and bought eye hook locks to place on the outside of both doors. He now locks his mother inside whenever he leaves and he hides the phones. Agnes complained about this treatment but quickly shut up when Peter once again threatened to place her in a nursing home if she said one more word.

Agnes can't eat, she can't sleep, she sits around staring at the four walls wondering how much longer she will have to endure this miserable life. A church elder stopped by one day to check up on her. Peter controlled much of the conversation, and when Peter got up to go to the bathroom Agnes told the elder what was going on. The church leader shrugged his shoulder and told her that she was laying up treasure in heaven by taking care of her son and providing a home for him.

Children who live in a house where there is psychological abuse are prone to behavior problems at school, have anxiety, depression and could likely suffer from post-traumatic stress disorder. In fact, if you were wondering if children suffer in the home where intimate partner violence exists, consider the following information:

This is from an article I saved from *USA Today* and it appeared on Monday, February 9, 1998. It was written by Marilyn Elias of *USA Today*: ***"Violent home is war zone for kids Study: Stress is*** *similar to soldiers' - Children who witness domestic violence often show life-impairing stress symptoms similar to those of combat war veterans, suggests a new study of Michigan families. Signs of intrusive remembering, such as 'flashbacks,' nightmares and compulsive re-enacting of the violence in play, were experienced by 52% of the children studied, says psychologist Sandra Graham-Bermann of the University of Michigan, Ann Arbor.*

Some 48% of the youngsters acted more irritable and angry since the violence, and 42% had trouble paying attention at school, mothers of the 64 children said.

It's one of the largest and most careful studies ever done of how kids are affected by seeing their mothers physically attacked by spouses or partners, says Jeffrey Edelson, a domestic violence expert at the University of Minnesota, Minneapolis. Violent acts had taken place in the last year: child witnesses were 7 to 12 years old."

The same paper had a companion article also written by Marilyn Elias of *USA Today.*

*"A place for kids from violent homes, by Marilyn Elias, **USA Today.** A small boy slammed his toy car into the wall – over and over and over. As psychologist Sandra Graham-Bermann watched him compulsively repeat the act, it made perfect sense. He'd recently seen his dad try to pin his mother against a wall with a car.*

Graham-Bermann has watched plenty of dolls get smashed too. When children witness violence between their parents, 'often they can't stop playing it out. They can't understand it, they're trying to master it, but they can't let it go until they make some sense of what happened,' she says.

The Kids Club, her group therapy program for kids from violent homes, has touched about 500 youngsters since it began as a pioneering experiment eight years ago in suburban Detroit. There are several similar U.S. programs now, most launched in the last few years, says psychologist Jeffrey Edelson, a family violence expert at the University of Minnesota, Minneapolis.

Still, there's far too little help for children affected by parental battling, experts agree. 'These child witnesses are a very important and unrecognized victim population,' says David Finkelhor of the University of New Hampshire's Family Research Laboratory.

Hard numbers on how many kids in the USA witness domestic violence don't exist. But national surveys on spousal battering suggest several million children see adult physical assaults at home every year.

Mounting studies show these children, overall, are more anxious, angry, depressed and mentally distracted than youngsters from homes without adult violence. They are also more likely to physically assault classmates, even at the preschool level.

Perhaps underrecognized is how frightened and worried many of these kids are, Graham-Bermann says, and how much their acting out may spring from a drive to master their own terror by at least controlling someone nearby.

Her recent study of 121 children 7 to 12 years old finds those with battered mothers are far more worried about the vulnerability of their moms and siblings, and the harmful behavior of fathers, than children whose mothers weren't assaulted.

Also, their anxiety and depression levels are closely linked to worry about fathers doing harm. 'These children may lash out at others as a way of controlling or stemming their own fears,' she says. But ending youngsters' exposure to violence can help them regain mental health, says Graham-Bermann, a University of Michigan faculty member. Some studies show the longer the time since a violent episode the fewer effects a child experiences.

And there are children who fare surprisingly well in violent families. Highly intelligent, adaptable children with strong interests and other supportive adults around may be best equipped to survive with minimal damage, Finkelhor says.

Groups such as the Kids Club also might help. A preliminary evaluation of the 10 week program, funded by Centers for Disease Control and Prevention, shows it improves children's mental health and social behavior, Graham-Bermann says.

Seventeen 'model' U.S. programs for battered women and their kids will be profiled this spring in a book published by the National Council of Juvenile and Family Court Judges. A woman who recently left a 17-year marriage to a violent man says she saw great progress in her children after they went to Kids Club. Her 9-year old son finally could be open about what happened and it comforted him to talk to other children. And she says her 11-year old daughter was less scared after the group. Both children learned a lot about domestic violence, she says. Their ability to concentrate and work at school improved too.

Post-traumatic stress disorder (PTSD) symptoms similar to those of war veterans aren't surprising in these youngsters, Finkelhor says, since all research on exposure to violence – from gang battles to inter-ethnic warfare – finds stress disorders are a common outcome. PTSD victims, 'have overwhelming levels of fear and helplessness,' feelings that may be familiar to some children who smash their dolls at the Kids Club.

And they are caught in crossfire from a hidden form of combat. Graham-Berman believes 'It's the war within the family.'"

The article ends with this information:

"How children are affected

Children's ages greatly influence how they react to violence between adults at home. Some typical effects are presented in a recent summary by violence experts Janis Wolak and David Finkelhor of the Family Research Laboratory at the University of New Hampshire, Durham.

Infants through age 5

- *If mother is injured or stressed, babies may show signs of health problems and neglect – underweight, inconsolable crying, etc.*

- *Preschoolers, particularly boys, often behave aggressively with peers. Whiny, clingy behavior or regression in toilet training are common. The child may appear anxious or sad.*

Ages 6 to 12

- *Aggressive behavior at school is a common problem.*

- *May act fearful, depressed or have low self-esteem.*

- *Can appear socially isolated, because they're ashamed to bring friends home or are restricted by a domineering parent.*

Adolescents

- *More prone than other teens to delinquency and physical assaults, particularly if they've spent many years in violent homes.*

- *May escape by running away. Some use drugs and alcohol to escape. Suicide is a concern for those who are withdrawn and depressed.*

- *Others stay home and assume parenting duties for younger siblings."*

Here are some statistics from the National Center for Children Exposed to Violence:

- Children who witness violence at home display emotional and behavioral disturbances as diverse as withdrawal, low self-esteem, nightmares, and aggression against peers, family members and property. *(Peled, Inat, Jaffe, Peter G. & Edelson, Jeffrey*

L. (eds.) Ending the Cycle of Violence: Community Responses to Children of Battered Women. Thousand Oaks, California: Sage Publications, 1995.)

- Over 3 million children are at risk of exposure to parental violence each year. *(Carlson, B.E. "Children's Observations of Interparental Violence" In Edwards, A.R. (ed.) Battered Women and Their Families. New York: Springer, Pp. 147-167. 1984.)*

- In a national survey of over 6,000 American families, 50 percent of the men who frequently assaulted their wives also frequently abused their children. *(Straus, M.A. & Gelles, R.J. (eds.) Physical violence in American families. New Brunswick, NJ, Transaction Publishers. 1990.)*

- In 1995, the FBI reported that 27 percent of all violent crime involves family on family violence, 48 percent involved acquaintances with the violence often occurring in the home. *(National Incident-Based Reporting System, Uniform Crime Reporting Program, 1999.)*

- Straus and Gelles (1996) have estimated that over 29 million children commit an act of violence against a sibling each year. *(Straus, M. & Gelles, R. 1998. How violent are American families: estimates from the national family violence survey and other studies. In: Family Abuse and its Consequences: New Directions in Research (G. Hotaling, et al., Eds.))*

- Studies show that child abuse occurs in 30 to 60 percent of family violence cases that involve families with children. *("The overlap between child maltreatment and woman beating." J.L. Edelson, Violence Against Women, February, 1999.)*

According to the National Coalition Against Domestic Violence (NCADV):

"Men, as well as women, are victimized by violence. Male victims are less likely than women to report violence and seek services due to the following challenges: the stigma of being a male victim, the failure to

conform to the macho stereotype, being perceived as a wimp, not being believed, being denied the status of victim, and lack of support from society, family members, and friends." (FORGE: For Ourselves: Reworking Gender Expression, Accessed July 2007 http://forge-forward.org.)

The NCADV website also states:

- One out of five women and one out of fourteen men has been physically assaulted by an intimate partner at some time in their lives. *(Thoennes, N., & Tjaden, P. (2000). Full Report of the Prevalence, Incidence, and Consequences of Violence Against Women; Findings from the National Violence Against Women Survey. National Institute of Justice and Centers for Disease Control and Prevention.)*

- 3.2 million men are physically assaulted annually in the United States. 26 percent of those assaults were attributed to intimate partner violence. *(Same source as above.)*

- According to the National Center for Victims of Crime, men experience many of the same psychological reactions to violence as women. Those include: guilt, shame, humiliation, anger, anxiety, depression and withdrawal from relationships. *(The National Center for Victims of Crime (1997) Male Rape.)*

- Men who witnessed domestic violence as children are twice as likely to abuse their own partners and children than those who did not witness domestic violence. *(Straus, M., et al. (1990). Physical Violence in American Families: Risk Factors and Adaptations to violence in 8,145 Families. New Brunswick: Transaction Publishers.)*

- Because men are more likely to be financially independent and less likely to experience fear upon leaving a violent relationship, men are less likely to seek emergency shelter services. *(Hamberger, L.K., & Guse, C. (2002). "Men's and Women's Use of Intimate Partner Violence in Clinical Samples." Violence Against Women, 8(11), 1301-1331.)*

- 86 percent of men who were physically assaulted since age 18 were physically assaulted by a man.

  70 percent of men who were raped since age 18 were raped by a male.

  56 percent of men who reported being physically assaulted were assaulted by a stranger, while 17 percent were assaulted by a current or former spouse, cohabitating partner, boyfriend/ girlfriend or date. *(Thoennes, N. & Tjaden, P. (2000). Full Report of the Prevalence, Incidence, and Consequences of Violence Against Women; Findings from the National Violence Against Women Survey. National Institute of Justice and Centers for Disease Control and Prevention.)*

- In a Bureau of Justice Statistics 2004 report, 5.5 percent of male homicide victims were murdered by a spouse, ex-spouse, boyfriend or girlfriend. *(Fox, J.A. & Zawitz, M.W. (2004). Homicide Trends in the U.S.: Trends by Gender. Bureau of Justice Statistics: Accessed July 2007 http://www.ojp.usdoj.gov/bjs/Homicide/gender.htm.)*

Let's look at just how lethal domestic violence can become. According to the F.B.I., the following is a Supplementary Homicide Report, listing victims by gender, who were all killed as a result of Intimate Partner incidents (the report was released June 29, 2006 and spans from 1976 to 2004):

YEAR	MALE	FEMALE	TOTAL	CHANGE	%CHANGE
1976	1348	1596	2944		
1977	1288	1430	2718	-226	-7.7%
1978	1193	1480	2673	-45	-1.7%
1979	1260	1506	2766	93	3.5%
1980	1217	1546	2763	-3	-0.1%
1981	1268	1567	2835	72	2.6%
1982	1135	1480	2615	-220	-7.8%
1983	1112	1461	2573	-42	-1.6%
1984	988	1439	2427	-146	-5.7%

YEAR	MALE	FEMALE	TOTAL	CHANGE	%CHANGE
1985	956	1546	2502	75	3.1%
1986	979	1584	2563	61	2.5%
1987	927	1486	2413	-150	-5.9%
1988	848	1578	2426	13	0.5%
1989	895	1411	2306	-120	-4.9%
1990	853	1493	2346	40	1.7%
1991	773	1503	2276	-70	-3.0%
1992	718	1448	2166	-110	-4.8%
1993	698	1571	2269	103	4.8%
1994	684	1403	2087	-182	-8.0%
1995	544	1315	1859	-228	-10.9%
1996	506	1310	1816	-43	-2.3%
1997	445	1209	1654	-162	-8.9%
1998	502	1310	1812	158	9.6%
1999	418	1204	1622	-190	-10.5%
2000	425	1238	1663	41	2.5%
2001	392	1194	1586	-77	-4.6%
2002	378	1193	1571	-15	-0.9%
2003	371	1163	1534	-37	-2.4%
2004	385	1159	1544	10	0.7%
TOTAL VICTIMS	23506	40823	64329		

There are no statistics yet for 2005 or 2006, but we can see that intimate partner violence is still a very real threat to people. While there are still male murder victims, the number has declined over the years and there haven't been more than 500 male victims since 1998. And, while the number of female murder victims has also declined, the total number killed has not dropped below 1159 since 1976.

As I am writing this book, I just read today, November 24, 2007, about a sad case in Maryland. Police were patrolling a secluded park area and saw two vehicles parked with engines running. In one car was a mom and her children, shot to death. Next to the other car was the father and estranged husband of the woman. He was found dead, laying on the ground from a self-inflicted gun shot wound. The park was their designated exchange location of their children for visitation purposes.

The numbers that we read do not even include the countless other victims including the children, aunts, uncles, other in-laws and even co-workers of the victims who were also killed by the abuser because they happened to be in the same area as the intended victim of the intimate partner murder/suicide.

If you want to see what the IPV female homicide rate for your state was in 2002, here are those statistics which show the number of homicides and the ranking of the state by numbers of women killed per 100,000 population.

Ranking	State	Number of Homicides
10	Alabama	42
1	Alaska	15
22	Arizona	36
11	Arkansas	25
20	California	239
14	Colorado	38
15	Connecticut	10
8	Delaware	9
	Florida	NA
17	Georgia	70
23	Hawaii	8
31 (tie)	Idaho	7
42	Illinois	43
25 (tie)	Indiana	38
40	Iowa	11

Ranking	State	Number of Homicides
37	Kansas	11
46	Kentucky	11
2	Louisiana	67
39	Maine	5
18	Maryland	45
45	Massachusetts	18
21	Michigan	68
38	Minnesota	20
15 (tie)	Mississippi	25
15 (tie)	Missouri	49
36	Montana	4
43	Nebraska	5
4	Nevada	27
48	New Hampshire	2
31 (tie)	New Jersey	46
3	New Mexico	25
25 (tie)	New York	120
9	North Carolina	88
34	North Dakota	3
27	Ohio	68
13	Oklahoma	31
41	Oregon	12
24	Pennsylvania	78
29 (tie)	Rhode Island	6
6	South Carolina	49
49	South Dakota	0
7	Tennessee	67
12	Texas	197
28	Utah	13

Ranking	State	Number of Homicides
47	Vermont	1
19	Virginia	53
29 (tie)	Washington	33
33	West Virginia	9
35	Wisconsin	26
5	Wyoming	6

Alaska ranked number one with a rate of 4.84 murders per 100,000 population. California had the highest number of homicides with 239 while Vermont had only one homicide in 2002.

Fifty four percent of these female homicides were committed with a firearm, and of those firearm homicides 73 percent were committed with handguns and 287 of these victims were shot and killed during the course of an argument. Homicides in which race was identified included: 15 American Indians or Alaskan Natives, 53 Asian or Pacific Islanders, 636 African American females and 1,159 white females.

So, now we know what Domestic Violence is, what laws are associated with Domestic Violence, the effects violence has on the victim and the children in the home, how intimate partner violence impacts the workplace, and we have seen just how volatile and deadly Domestic Violence is. We can see that it is a huge problem, and since we know that 1 in 4 women have been or currently are living in a violent home, we can assume that 25 percent of the women in your church congregation are also victims of intimate partner violence.

We also know that there can be many acts of violence before the victim ever calls the police or confides in a family member or friend to even disclose that they are a victim of abuse.

So when the victim gets up the courage to finally ask a church leader for help, that church leader is the first line of defense for that victim and the response of that church leader will determine whether or not that victim will be safe, or exposed to many more years of violence or even death.

There are usually three different scenarios between victim and abuser:

Scenario #1
- Victim attends church with her children, husband is a non-believer, but may attend church twice a year – Easter and Christmas Eve.

Scenario #2
- Victim and abuser both attend church regularly and abuser even claims to be a believer.

Scenario #3
- Victim and abuser both attend church regularly and abuser is even a deacon, elder, pastor, choir director or Sunday School Teacher.

In the first situation, if the pastor, priest, elder or deacon tells the victim: "Your job is to be a good wife and a good mother, go home and be obedient," that victim will just continue to endure the violence and could end up being killed some day. If the church leader says, "O.K., I'll go over and talk to your husband, maybe I can talk some sense into him," this is a bad idea, because what will usually happen is the abuser will become very hostile and irate. To abusers, their abuse at home is their "little secret," and they expect the victim and the children to keep it the "family secret." Abusers know that what they are doing is wrong. They would be highly embarrassed if ANYONE knew what they were doing. The likely outcome of the meeting with the abuser will be the abuser denying, minimizing, telling the church leader that this is no one's business. After the meeting the victim will likely be subjected to a very harsh beating and the abuser will threaten her and tell her that if she ever tells anyone else about what is going on at home she will die. The abuser will also more than likely tell the victim that she can no longer attend church. So, the abuser will hide her car keys on Saturday night, and he will not allow her to call her friends from church. So the victim loses out in so many ways, she feels more at risk, and the one thing in her life that she looked forward to each week – going to church – will be stripped from her.

With scenario two, if the abuser comes to church every Sunday with his wife and kids, knows quite a few people, maybe volunteers at Vacation Bible School, maybe even teaches a Sunday School class, and if the pastor or elder goes to approach him, the outcome will not be much different than in scenario one. He will become angry, deny the allegation or minimize it, or tell them, "She just knows how to push my buttons!" The abuser will tell them that it's none of their business and he will confront the victim, ask her why she told, and demand to know how many more people she has told. He will either withdraw to the point where he no longer volunteers, he may quit attending church for several weeks or months, or he most likely will announce that he and his family are withdrawing their membership in the church. He will demand that the whole family start trying out new churches. The victim is also in great peril because the abuser will be very angry that she told, and it could lead to more violence.

Scenario three will mock the behaviors in scenario two, except the elder, deacon or pastor will probably not step down from the leadership role, they will deny the accusations or downplay them. The victim is probably at a greater risk of violence than the victims in the first two scenarios, because of pride, and appearances of the accused church leader, and he will now have to do some sort of damage control to make himself look good. The church leader who is accused may also get angry, pull his family's church membership and move onto a new church where "no one knows."

As a church elder, I have seen all three of these scenarios go these ways. I have also talked to church leaders of other churches who have reported the same outcomes. It is very rare that you get an abuser in any one of these three situations to have a contrite heart, acknowledge that what they have been doing was wrong, and then take the steps to change the behavior.

Danny is 15 and his dad and mom are very active in their church. He has a 13 year old sister, and his dad has served two, three-year terms as a church elder. The elder board had asked him to stay on for another term, but Ray said that he wanted to take some time off. Danny has a friend at church, Chris, who is also 15, and he invited Danny to sleep over on Friday night. While Danny was over at Chris', Danny started crying and told Chris that his dad beats him, his sister and his mom. Danny says that he doesn't know what to do. He can't tell his youth pastor – "my dad hired the youth pastor, my dad has gone to many meetings and elder/pastor retreats with our youth pastor." Chris wants to help so he tells his mom. His mom is flabbergasted, she cannot believe what she is hearing, but she does believe Danny, especially after he told her what has happened. She noticed how trembling and shaken he was as he recounted incident after incident of violent episodes at home.

Chris' mom calls the senior pastor. It's almost midnight and she tells the pastor everything. The pastor can hardly believe what he is hearing and says, "This is impossible. Ray has been an elder, he's a trusted friend and, well, haven't you seen him at worship time? Most often he is the only one standing while the praise band is playing." Chris' mom insists that the pastor go talk to Ray and the pastor refuses. He says, "I tell you what, I know Danny pretty well. I'll be over to talk to him in the morning before you have to bring him back home."

The next day, at 8:15 a.m., the pastor stops over and talks to Danny. "Having some problems at home I hear?" he says to the teen. Danny nods his head up and down. Danny gets up the courage to share some of the incidents, and the pastor says, "You know, Danny, I know your dad very well, and I just find it hard to believe that what you are telling me is true." Danny bursts into tears and runs to the kitchen. He is crying and saying, "I knew it, I knew I shouldn't have said anything. I knew no one would believe me!"

The pastor now feels badly and, for the first time, begins to think that there just may be some truth in what Danny is saying. But the pastor tells Chris' mom, "I'm just too close to Ray. I tell you what, what time were you supposed to bring Danny home today?" "Umm, about 2:15," she replies. "O.K., well you know Will from church, he's a police officer. He is off today, so I'll see if he can just meet you over there when you drop Danny off. We'll let Will confront Ray about this stuff."

So, at 2:15, she takes Danny home and Will is waiting half way down the block. He pulls up to the house and walks up the front sidewalk with Danny, Chris and Chris' mom. Before they can even ring the doorbell, Ray opens the door and says, "Hi everyone, how was your sleep over, Danny? And, Will, why are you here?" Will says, "Can we all come in and talk to you?" "DANNY! What did you do?" Ray asks sternly, because he thinks Danny is in some trouble. Why else would an off-duty police officer from church be here? As they all sit down in the living room, Ray's wife and daughter also walk in and Will says, "You see, Ray, Danny isn't in any trouble. He just expressed some concerns to Chris' mom about a few things going on here at home." "Like what?!" Ray asks in a demanding tone. "Well, Danny said that there are some physically abusive things going on here and he says that you are doing things to him, his sister and his mom." Ray stands up, extends his left arm out real quick and, with a pointed index finger, says, "DANNY! GET UP TO YOUR ROOM NOW!" Danny starts to get up, Chris' mom says, "Danny sit down, you don't have to go to your room." Ray says to Chris' mom, "Listen here you meddling b----! I'm not going to stand for having you tell Danny or anyone else in my house what they do or don't have to do!"

Chris' mom is upset now and yells, "I can't believe you just called me that name, I'm surprised! Some Christian you are!" Ray's wife is crying, his daughter buries her face into her hands and runs to her room. Ray yells at Danny, "Didn't I tell you to get to your room!" So Danny goes off to his room, and Ray yells at Chris' mom, Chris and Will, "You three can leave! Get out of here and Danny is not going to be staying over at your house ever again!" Will says, "Now, Ray, just try to calm down, we just want to help." "WELL, YOUR HELP IS NOT NEEDED AND NOT WANTED SO GET OUT!!" Ray yells. As they are leaving, Ray asks, "How many other people have you told these lies to?" Chris' mom says, "Look, Danny was crying, I called pastor, and he called Will." "YOU TOLD PASTOR?! That's just great! Get out now!"

No formal report is ever made at the police department when Will goes back to work. Social Services is never called so that they can follow up with a home visit. Ray calls the pastor and the pastor tells him that due to the nature of the allegations someone had to look into it. Ray told his family to keep their mouths shut, and no one knows for sure what kinds of abuse were occurring, and no one knows if any of it ever ended.

But in church this is how the church has historically handled reports of abuse. The church tries to handle it all "in house" without involving anyone else. The church leaders, while good intentioned, try to downplay the whole thing in an effort to not "offend" the abuser because, after all, we wouldn't want them to get mad and quit going to church. And it isn't all Will's fault. He is good friends with the pastor, and the pastor thought that Will would be able to use his experience in dealing with family trouble calls to make a positive intervention. And when the pastor called Will, it was implied that this would be Will intervening and not an actual "police response" so as not to concern or offend Ray.

Now, let's say that Will had been able to involve his police department. He and his department could have had Danny make a taped, one-party consent phone call to his dad. (In Wisconsin and most other states, it is legal and a great investigative tool, the caller knows that the phone conversation is being taped and the receiving party does not.) Danny could have told his dad that he isn't coming home, and that he is uncomfortable at home because of the physical abuse that he is inflicting on his sister, his mom and him. He could have asked his dad, "Why do you do these things to us?" Ray then may have made many confessions about the abuse on tape, charges could have been filed, possibly an arrest made, and something positive and lasting could have come of the whole situation. Instead, Ray was able to protect himself, he was able to keep his secret, and we have no idea how much more abuse the rest of the family was subjected to.

If you are pastor, an elder or a deacon you are a church leader. You are a shepherd of the flock. Think for a moment about how a shepherd takes care of his flock. In Psalm 78:52 it says, "But he brought his people out like a flock; he led them like sheep through the desert," (NIV). And the King James reads: "But made his own people to go forth like sheep, and guided them in the wilderness like a flock." This passage is showing God's care for his people when they were delivered from Egypt, and demonstrates the care and love that a shepherd has.

Psalm 100.3 (KJV) reads, "Know ye that the Lord he is God: it is he that hath made us, and we not ourselves; we are his people, and the sheep of his pasture." This shows us how much intimate care shepherds have for their flock.

In Acts 20:28, Paul is speaking to the elders of the church and tells them: "Keep watch over yourselves and all the flock of which the Holy spirit has made you overseers. Be shepherds of the church of God, which he bought with his own blood," (NIV). And in the King James: "Take heed therefore unto yourselves, and to all the flock, over which the Holy Ghost hath made you overseers, to feed the church of God, which he hath purchased with his own blood."

Now ask yourself, as priest, pastor, bishop, elder or deacon, can there be anything more important than being an overseer of a flock, bought with God's own blood?

Read 1 Peter 5:1-4, "To the elders among you, I appeal as a fellow elder, a witness of Christ's sufferings and one who also will share in the glory to be revealed; Be shepherds of God's flock that is under your care, serving as overseers – not because you must, but because you are willing, as God wants you to be; not greedy for money, but eager to serve, not lording it over those entrusted to you, but being examples to the flock. And when the Chief Shepherd appears, you will receive the crown of glory that will never fade away," (NIV). And in the King James: "The elders which are among you I exhort, who am also an elder, and a witness of the sufferings of Christ, and also a partaker of the glory that shall be revealed: Feed the flock of God which is among you, taking the oversight thereof, not by constraint, but willingly, not for filthy lucre, but of ready mind; Neither as being lords over God's heritage but being examples to the flock."

And if you are wondering what will happen to sheep without a shepherd, read Jeremiah 50:6 (NIV), "My people have been lost sheep; their shepherds have led them astray and caused them to roam on the mountains. They wandered over the mountains and hill and forgot their own resting place." And in verse 7 we read, of the sheep without a shepherd, "whoever found them devoured them." And in the King James Version: "My people hath been lost sheep: their shepherds have caused them to go astray, they have turned them away on the mountains, they have gone from mountain to hill, they have forgotten their resting place."

Ezekiel had sharp words for shepherds who had neglected the flock in chapter 34 verses 4 through 6: "You (shepherds) have not strengthened the weak or healed the sick or bound up the injured. You have not brought back the strays or searched for the lost . . . so they were scattered because there was no shepherd, and when they were scattered they became food for all the wild animals. My sheep wandered over all the mountains and on every high hill. They were scattered over the whole earth, and no one searched or looked for them," (NIV).

How about the care of the flock that Jesus modeled: Matthew 9:36, "When he saw the crowds, he had compassion on them, because they were harassed and helpless, like sheep without a shepherd," (NIV). And in the King James: "But when he saw the multitudes, he was moved with compassion on them, because they fainted, and were scattered abroad, as sheep having no shepherd."

And before Jesus ascended into heaven, he met with Peter and had this conversation: John 21:15-17: "When they finished eating, Jesus said to Simon Peter, 'Simon son of John, do you truly love me more than these?' 'Yes Lord,' he said, 'You know that I love you.' Jesus said, 'Feed my lambs.' Again Jesus said, 'Simon son of John, do you truly love me?' He answered, 'Yes Lord, you know that I love you.' Jesus said, 'Take care of my sheep.' The third time he said to him, 'Simon son of John, do you love me?' Peter was hurt because Jesus asked him the third time, 'Do you love me?' He said, 'Lord you know all things, you know that I love you.' Jesus said, 'Feed my sheep.'"

Jesus kept asking Peter because the word "love" that Jesus was asking was a total commitment to Christ and taking care of the sheep. Peter kept answering in a word that meant love, but not a total commitment type of "love," probably because Peter was remembering that he himself, just a short time ago, denied Christ three times after Jesus was arrested. But look at the command of Jesus, "feed my lambs, take care of my sheep, feed my sheep."

Jesus used many references about sheep and a shepherd, but look now at John 10:1-4: (NIV), "I tell you the truth, the man who does not enter the sheep pen by the gate, but climbs in by some other way is a thief and a robber. The man who enters by the gate is the shepherd of his sheep. The watchman opens the gate for him, and the sheep listen to his voice. He calls his own sheep by name and calls them out. When he has brought out all of his own he goes ahead of them, and his sheep follow him because they know his voice."

Jesus went on to explain in verse 7 because the disciples did not understand what he was telling them. What he was saying was that he is the gate for the sheep, all who ever came before Jesus were thieves and robbers, and since Jesus is the gate, whoever enters through him will be saved.

In John 10:11-13, Jesus said, "I am the good shepherd. The good shepherd lays down his life for his sheep. The hired hand is not the shepherd who owns the sheep. So when he sees the wolf coming he abandons the sheep and runs away. Then the wolf attacks the flock and scatters it. The man runs away because he is a hired hand and cares nothing for the sheep." (NIV).

So, as pastors, priests, elders and deacons, it is very clear that these are not only preaching and teaching positions, and not just leadership positions, but rather nurturing and caring positions, and that the congregation is the flock. And since Jesus ascended into heaven, he has given over the job of shepherd and overseer to trusted, caring people here on earth. And if you serve in such a capacity, you are a shepherd, and your congregation is your flock.

And if you want to get even a better picture of how a shepherd cares for sheep, take a look now at King David, a man who really knew what it meant to care for a flock. David wrote one of the most memorized and recited passages in Psalm 23 (KJV):

"The Lord is my shepherd, I shall not want." There aren't many things that sheep can do for themselves. They are basically defenseless animals who need protection from predators. They need someone to lead them to a grazing area, and someone to watch over them at night to protect them while they sleep.

"He maketh me lie down in green pastures; he leadeth me beside the still waters." A good shepherd knows when to find water for the flock, especially when you are in the desert. A shepherd knows that the sheep need good, green grass to eat. A caring shepherd would not lead them to a thistle patch.

"He restoreth my soul; he leadeth me in paths of righteousness for his names' sake." I like Eugene Peterson's Message Bible version: **"True to your word, you let me catch my breath and send me in the right direction."** This shows God's grace and perfect guidance. Sheep tend to wander and when David was a shepherd, there was no barbed wire to keep them in one area. I'm sure David had to run ahead of them, to gently guide them in the right direction.

"**Yea, though I walk through the valley of the shadow of death, I will fear no evil; for thou art with me; thy rod and thy staff they comfort me.**" Again, Eugene Peterson's Message Bible makes the point even better: "**Even when the way goes through Death Valley, I'm not afraid when you walk at my side. Your trusty shepherd's crook makes me feel secure.**" I can imagine David out with his flock, when he is passing by an area where there were wild animals who were predators, or approaching with his flock towards men who may be thieves. I can just see him scanning the area and making sure that nothing would happen to even one of his flock. I did some research on sheep and found out that a shepherd would use the staff to block a dangerous path, or to place in front of the face of a sheep to keep it from eating poison ivy. I talked to a guy that I know who raises sheep. He said that some of his sheep got into the barn somehow, and they chewed a bag of corn, got it open and started eating the corn until they had eaten so much that several died and the rest were sick. They were sick from an overdose of protein that they received from the corn. A shepherd would have done whatever he could to keep the sheep from harm, and that shepherd's crook would be a source of correction and love.

"**Thou preparest a table before me in the presence of mine enemies; thou anointest my head with oil; my cup runneth over.**" There's this picture of God the shepherd, being a generous provider, and throughout the Bible anointing with oil goes hand-in-hand with blessings. I learned another thing about shepherds of old, they would put oil on the faces of their sheep to protect them from biting snakes while the flock was grazing in the thick grass.

"**Surely goodness and mercy shall follow me all the days of my life; and I will dwell in the house of the Lord forever.**" There is this idea that the intimate fellowship and protection from God the shepherd will never end.

Psalm 23 could only be written by a shepherd, about how shepherds care for their sheep, and David was the best person to write this as he himself had spent many years looking after and caring for sheep.

Look at David as a teenager in 1 Samuel 17. David's older brothers are all at the Philistine battle lines where the huge Goliath is coming forward and taunting King Saul and his men for 40 days. In verses 17-20, "Now Jesse said to his son David, 'Take his ephah' (probably about half a bushel) 'of roasted grain and these ten loaves of bread for your brothers, and hurry to their camp. Take along these ten cheeses to the commander of their unit. See how your brothers are and bring back some assurance from them. They are with Saul and all men of Israel in the Valley of Elah, fighting against the Philistines.' Early in the morning David left the flock with a shepherd," (notice that he just didn't take off and leave his sheep on their own to fend for themselves – that's what shepherds do, even in their absence they provide), "loaded up and set out, as Jesse had directed. He reached the camp as the army was going out to its battle positions, shouting the war cry," (NIV).

Now David noticed that Goliath was taunting the army of Israel and he was also seeing that no one in Saul's army was about to go up against Goliath. In 1 Samuel 17:32-38 we read: "David" (this little teenager) "said to Saul, 'Let no one lose heart on account of this Philistine; your servant will go and fight him.' Saul replied, 'You are not able to go out against this Philistine and fight him; you are only a boy, and he has been a fighting man from his youth.' But David said to Saul, 'Your servant has been keeping his father's sheep. When a lion or bear came and carried off a sheep from the flock, I went after it, struck it and rescued the sheep from its mouth. When it turned on me, I seized it and killed it. Your servant has killed both the lion and the bear; this uncircumcised Philistine will be like one of them, because he has defied the armies of the living God. The Lord who delivered me from the paw of the lion and the paw of the bear will deliver me from the hand of this Philistine.' Saul said to David, 'Go, and the Lord be with you.'"

David goes to the battle lines, no armor, just his staff in his hand, five smooth stones from the stream and his sling. In verses 41-44 (NIV) we read: "Meanwhile, the Philistine, with his shield bearer in front of him, kept coming closer to David. He looked David over and saw that he was only a boy, ruddy and handsome, and he despised him. He said to David, 'Am I a dog, that you come at me with sticks?' And the Philistine cursed David by his gods. 'Come here,' he said, 'and I'll give your flesh to the birds of the air and the beasts of the field!'"

Verses 48-50 continue the story: "As the Philistine moved closer to attack him, David ran quickly toward the battle line to meet him. Reaching into his bag and taking out a stone, he slung it and struck the Philistine on the forehead, and he fell facedown on the ground. So David triumphed over the Philistine with a sling and a stone; without a sword in his hand he struck down the Philistine and killed him," (NIV).

Notice that David not only had confidence that God would assure him the victory, but David also drew his confidence from being a shepherd and rescuing his father's sheep from lions and bears. I can just see David, out in the desert, chasing after a predator and taking the sheep back from the attacker. I also see David sitting on a rock, looking over his sheep, singing, and having regular target practice with his sling and some stones as he passed the many lonely hours that he spent looking after the sheep.

I asked my sheep raising friend if sheep will attack other sheep in the flock. He said that Rams, the male sheep, will fight with one another, and if the shepherd does not intervene and separate them, they will head butt one another until one or both dies. I asked him if male sheep attack or kill female sheep. He replied that during the mating season he knows when all of the sheep have been mated when a ram will become a little aggressive towards a ewe who has already mated and is no longer interested in the ram. But, he said, the ram will not harm or kill a female sheep.

So, you see that the shepherds – priests, pastors, elders and deacons – want to treat the offending, attacking male sheep of the church flock, as a co-sheep, even a co-offending sheep, when the female sheep of the church flock is being battered and bruised, but we know from our research of sheep, that the ram does not attack or kill a female sheep.

So, church leaders who are charged with the care of the flock need to see the abuser for who he or she is: a lion or a bear, and church leaders need to go after that lion or bear and free the sheep from its paws. But most church leaders are more content to play it safe and say, "Well, we'll be praying for you," or, "Your job is to be a good mother and wife, go home and be obedient." And when shepherds tell their abused and broken sheep this, they leave the defenseless sheep and their lambs in the paws and jaws of those lions and bears.

Church leaders need to see the abuser for what he or she is. How could a ram be of the flock and still attack a ewe? Didn't Jesus say in the Book of John chapter 13 verses 34 and 35: "A new commandment I give unto you, That ye love one another; as I have loved you, that ye also love one another. By this shall all men know that ye are my disciples, if ye also have love one to another," (KJV). So, could or would a spouse act out in an abusive manner towards their spouse if they were trying to show the world that they loved that person and were trying to be a disciple of Christ. Couldn't we then say that if a person was abusing his or her spouse, and refused to stop the behaviors, and never repented of the abuse, that they are not committed to Christ and may not really be a Christian?

I found out some other interesting things about the care that shepherds have for their sheep. If a sheep somehow rolls over onto its back, because of their short little legs they cannot stand back up without the assistance of the shepherd. Shepherds of David's age did not have barns or fenced in areas to keep their sheep at night, so they made a pen out of stones. They had a short wall that went all the way around an area, and the gate area is where a shepherd would lay down so that no predators or thieves could walk in through the doorway. Isn't it interesting that Jesus said in John chapter 10 verses 1-4, "I tell you the truth, the man who does not enter the sheep pen by the gate, but climbs in by some other way is a thief and a robber. The man who enters by the gate is the shepherd of his sheep. The watchman opens the gate for him, and the sheep listen to his voice as he calls his own sheep by name and leads them out. When he has brought out all of his own, he goes on ahead of them, and his sheep follow him because they know his voice," (NIV).

So, as shepherds in our churches today, we do stand at the church doors greeting the flock. And in the same way as shepherds of old, do we notice if a sheep is limping, maybe it got injured that day out in the field? Are we noticing that one of the lambs has burrs in its fur and we pull it aside and take them out to make the lamb more comfortable? Are church leaders, like shepherds, laying down their lives at the gate of the pen to protect the sheep from wolves? Are church leaders, who deal with domestic violence issues, true shepherds or hired hands who run from the attacking wolf?

And, if you are wondering how important shepherds are to God, isn't it interesting that an angel went first to shepherds, watching over their flocks to announce the birth of Jesus (Luke 2:8), and not just any shepherds, but the lowly, late night, graveyard shift shepherds?

I heard Chuck Swindoll of the radio program "Insight For Living" say that the church is like a hospital. That one week some people in the congregation are in the emergency room, others are in the critical care unit. Some are in the heart wing, some are in surgery, others are in recovery and many others are just visitors. The following week, those who were in the critical care unit of life are still there, some are out, someone moved up to the recovery area from the emergency room of life, and those who were just visitors are now in the critical care unit. His point was so true, and any pastor, priest, elder, deacon or other church leader can tell you that they purposefully stand at the front doors of the church each week to meet and greet the people and to find out what the state of the flock is. As a church leader, do you see yourself as a shepherd of old, standing at the gate of the sheep pen, inspecting the sheep, making sure that those who need attention and care receive it? And when a woman walks up to you and tells you that her husband is violent, or you see a bruise or scratch, can you be a true caring shepherd if you just tell her to go home and be a good wife? Especially after reading what you have so far about abuse and how devastating it can be? In the next two chapters we will talk about dealing with the abuser and how to intervene on behalf of the victim.

When a sheep is a victim of domestic violence and makes his or her shepherd aware of their plight, that disclosure may be the one and only chance that the shepherd has to intervene. It is too easy to do nothing and move on, and when we let the victim know that no action will be taken, the problem is still there and escalating. The church response needs to be well thought through, and safety of the victim should be the number one priority. Care for the sheep should be the response of the church.

Chapter Five

Dealing With Nabal

A FRIEND OF MINE WAS overweight, he smoked, never exercised, and was only 42 years old. One night he was sitting in his easy chair, getting ready to go to bed, when he had sharp pains in his chest and back. He sat there for about 15 minutes before he finally convinced himself that this was not indigestion. This guy drove himself to the emergency room, and a good thing that he went. The attending physician told him that he had suffered a heart attack, and the next day several blocked arteries were cleaned out. Eight months later, he has lost most of his excess weight, he has stopped smoking, and he now jogs three times a week. My friend said to me, "Mark, that was a wake up call. I desperately needed a wake up call."

Two summers ago, my dispatcher sent me to a roll-over accident. A single car was going through a curve too fast. The car went off road right, flew over a guardrail, and the car rolled three times down a hill. The driver was injured severely and was pinned inside of her car. Had it not been for a passing newspaper deliverer, no one else would have witnessed this incident at 2:07 in the morning, and her car probably would not have been noticed by anyone until later that day.

Six months later I ran into this woman in the store, and she recognized me as being one of the officers who had responded and issued her for operating while intoxicated. She said to me, "This is going to sound strange, but I wanted to thank you for arresting me that night." She went on to say that she had been driving home drunk almost five nights a week that summer. She said, "That crash, and having to go to court changed me. Believe me, it was a wake up call." She told me that she had joined AA, and that she hadn't had anything to drink since that night.

Nabal needs a wake up call. Nothing changes if nothing changes, and in order to repair a marriage, in order to bring healing and to put an end to the abuse, Nabal does indeed need a wake up call. Nabal will be very resistant to change and for good reason. Who would want to give up always being right, having everything go their way, and having the final say in everything? Abusers love control, and if something or someone tries to take that away from them, get ready for a fight.

Nabal is going to deny, minimize and blame the abusive behavior. How he (or she) is approached can make the difference between a successful intervention, or a more dangerous, even deadly situation for the victim. Nabals also differ in how to be approached, and we will look now at the differences between Nabal the non-believer/Easter and Christmas only church attender, Nabal the regular attender/ church member, and Nabal the church leader.

Abigail told David in 1 Samuel 25:25, "May my lord pay no attention to that wicked man Nabal. He is just like his name – his name is Fool, and folly goes with him." So, Nabal is a fool which may explain why he acts as he does and should give us a prediction of how he/she will respond when confronted. Webster's American Dictionary defines fool as: "a person who lacks good judgment and common sense; a silly or stupid person." Folly is defined as: "a lack of good sense; foolishness, any foolish action, belief, etc." So we can see that we will be dealing with someone who is going to be difficult to get through to.

King David's son, King Solomon, also gives us some insight into how fools behave and how they will react. King Solomon wrote quite a bit in Proverbs about Fools and Foolishness. Let's take a look at these verses:

Proverbs 10:10b, ". . . and a chattering fool comes to ruin," (NIV).

Proverbs 10:14, "Wise men store up knowledge, but the mouth of a fool invites ruin," (NIV).

Proverbs 10:23, "A fool finds pleasure in evil conduct, but a man of understanding delights in wisdom," (NIV).

Proverbs 11:29, "He who brings trouble on his family will inherit only wind, and the fool will be servant to the wise," (NIV). Inherit the wind means that all he has will be blown away.

Proverbs 12:1, "Whoever loves discipline loves knowledge, but he who hates correction is stupid," (NIV).

Proverbs 12:15, "The way of a fool seems right to him, but a wise man listens to advice," (NIV).

Proverbs 12:18, "Reckless words pierce like a sword, but the tongue of the wise brings healing," (NIV).

Proverbs 12:20, "There is deceit in the hearts of those who plot evil, but joy for those who promote peace," (NIV).

Proverbs 13:10, "Pride only brings quarrels, but wisdom is found in those who take advice," (NIV).

Proverbs 14:1, "The wise woman builds her house, but with her own hands the foolish one tears hers down," (NIV).

Proverbs 14:2, "He whose walk is upright fears the Lord, but he whose ways are devious despises him," (NIV).

Proverbs 14:7, "Stay away from a foolish man, for you will not find knowledge on his lips," (NIV).

Proverbs 14:8, "The wisdom of the prudent is to give thought to their ways, but the folly of fools is deception," (NIV).

Proverbs 14:9, "Fools mock at making amends for sin, but good will is found among the upright," (NIV).

Proverbs 14:11, "The house of the wicked will be destroyed, but the tent of the upright will flourish," (NIV).

Proverbs 14:12, "There is a way that seems right to a man, but in the end it leads to death," (NIV).

Proverbs 14:14, "The faithless will be fully repaid for their ways, and the good man rewarded for his," (NIV).

Proverbs 14:16, "A wise man fears the Lord and shuns evil, but the fool is hotheaded and reckless," (NIV).

Proverbs 14:17, "A quick-tempered man does foolish things,"(NIV).

Proverbs 14:22, "Do not those who plot evil go astray? But those who plan what is good find love and faithfulness," (NIV).

Proverbs 15:1, "A gentle answer turns away wrath, but a harsh word stirs up anger," (NIV).

Proverbs 15:2, "The tongue of the wise commends knowledge, but the mouth of the fool gushes folly," (NIV).

Proverbs 15:4, "The tongue that brings healing is a tree of life, but a deceitful tongue crushes the spirit," (NIV).

Proverbs 15:5, "A fool spurns his father's discipline, but whoever heeds correction shows prudence," (NIV).

Proverbs 15:8, "The Lord detests the sacrifice of the wicked, but the prayer of the upright pleases him," (NIV).

Proverbs 15:9, "The Lord detests the way of the wicked but he loves those who pursue righteousness," (NIV).

Proverbs 15:12, "A mocker resents correction; he will not consult the wise," (NIV).

Proverbs 15:17, " Better a meal of vegetables where there is love than a fattened calf with hatred," (NIV).

Proverbs 15:18, "A hot-tempered man stirs up dissension, but a patient man calms a quarrel," (NIV).

Proverbs 15:19, "The way of the sluggard is blocked with thorns, but the path of the upright is a highway," (NIV).

Proverbs 15:29, "The Lord is far from the wicked but he hears the prayer of the righteous," (NIV).

Proverbs 16:18, "Pride goes before destruction . . ." (NIV).

Proverbs 17:11, "An evil man is bent only on rebellion; a merciless official will be sent against him," (NIV).

Proverbs 17:15, "Acquitting the guilty and condemning the innocent – the Lord detests them both," (NIV).

Proverbs 17:19, "He who loves a quarrel loves sin . . ." (NIV).

Proverbs 17:20, "A man of perverse heart does not prosper; he whose tongue is deceitful falls into trouble," (NIV).

Proverbs 17:21, "To have a fool for a son brings grief; there is no joy for the father of a fool," (NIV).

Proverbs 17:25, "A foolish son brings grief to his father and bitterness to the one who bore him," (NIV).

Proverbs 17:27, "A man of knowledge uses words with restraint, and a man of understanding is even-tempered," (NIV).

Proverbs 17:28, "Even a fool is thought wise if he keeps silent, and discerning if he holds his tongue," (NIV).

Proverbs 18:1, "An unfriendly man pursues selfish ends; he defies all sound judgment," (NIV).

Proverbs 18:2, "A fool finds no pleasure in understanding but delights in airing his own opinions," (NIV).

Proverbs 18:5, "It is not good to be partial to the wicked or to deprive the innocent of justice," (NIV).

Proverbs 18:6, "A fool's lips bring him strife, and his mouth invites a beating," (NIV).

Proverbs 18:7, "A fool's mouth is his undoing, and his lips are a snare to his soul," (NIV).

Proverbs 18:13, "He who answers before listening – that is his folly and his shame," (NIV).

Proverbs 18:17, "The first to present his case seems right, till another comes forward and questions him," (NIV).

Proverbs 18:22, "He who finds a wife finds what is good and receives favor from the Lord," (NIV).

Proverbs 19:5, "A false witness will not go unpunished, and he who pours out lies will not go free," (NIV).

Proverbs 19:11, "A man's wisdom gives him patience, it is to his glory to overlook an offense," (NIV).

Proverbs 19:13, "A foolish son is a father's ruin, and a quarrelsome wife is like a constant dripping," (NIV).

Proverbs 19:19, "A hot-tempered man must pay the penalty; if you rescue him, you will have to do it again," (NIV).

Proverbs 20:1, "Wine is a mocker and beer a brawler; whoever is led astray by either is not wise," (NIV).

Proverbs 20:3, "It is to a man's honor to avoid strife, but every fool is quick to quarrel," (NIV).

Proverbs 20:11, "Even a child is known by his actions, by whether his conduct is pure and right," (NIV).

Proverbs 21:23, "He who guards his mouth and his tongue keeps himself from calamity," (NIV).

Proverbs 21:29, "A wicked man puts up a bold front . . ." (NIV).

Proverbs 22:10, "Drive out the mocker, and out goes strife; quarrels and insults are ended," (NIV).

Proverbs 22:24, "Do not make friends with a hot-tempered man, do not associate with one easily angered, or you may learn his ways and get yourself ensnared," (NIV).

Proverbs 23:9, "Do not speak to a fool, for he will scorn the wisdom of your words," (NIV).

Proverbs 24:1, "Do not envy wicked men, do not desire their company; for their hearts plot violence, and their lips talk about making trouble," (NIV).

Proverbs 24:7, "Wisdom is too high for a fool, in the assembly at the gate he has nothing to say," (NIV).

Proverbs 24:8, "He who plots evil will be known as a schemer. The schemes of folly are sin, and men detest a mocker," (NIV).

Proverbs 26:4, "Do not answer a fool according to his folly, or you will be like him yourself," (NIV).

Proverbs 26:11, "As a dog returns to his vomit, so a fool repeats his folly," (NIV).

Proverbs 26:21, "As charcoal to embers and as wood to fire, so is a quarrelsome man for kindling strife," (NIV).

Proverbs 27:3, "Stone is heavy and sand a burden, but provocation by a fool is heavier than both," (NIV).

Proverbs 27:8, "Like a bird that strays from its nest is a man who strays from his home," (NIV).

Proverbs 27:12, "The prudent see danger and take refuge, but the simple keep going and suffer for it," (NIV).

Proverbs 27:22, "Though you grind a fool in a mortar, grinding him like grain with a pestle, you will not remove his folly from him," (NIV).

Proverbs 28:1, "The wicked man flees though no one pursues, but the righteous are as bold as a lion," (NIV).

Proverbs 28:5, "Evil men do not understand justice, but those who seek the Lord understand it fully," (NIV).

Proverbs 28:13, "He who conceals his sins does not prosper, but whoever confesses and renounces them finds mercy," (NIV).

Proverbs 28:15, "Like a roaring lion or a charging bear is a wicked man ruling over helpless people," (NIV).

Proverbs 28:23, "He who rebukes a man will in the end gain more favor than he who has a flattering tongue," (NIV).

Proverbs 28:26, "He who trusts in himself is a fool, but he who walks in wisdom is kept safe," (NIV).

Proverbs 29:1, "A man who remains stiff-necked after many rebukes will suddenly be destroyed – without remedy," (NIV).

Proverbs 29:9, "If a wise man goes to court with a fool, the fool rages and scoffs, and there is no peace," (NIV).

Proverbs 29:11, "A fool gives full vent to his anger, but a wise man keeps himself under control," (NIV).

Proverbs 29:22, "An angry man stirs up dissension, and a hot-tempered one commits many sins," (NIV).

Proverbs 29:23, "A man's pride brings him low, but a man of lowly spirit gains honor," (NIV).

Proverbs 30:33, "For as churning mills produces butter, and as twisting the nose produces blood, so stirring up anger produces strife," (NIV).

Anyone who says that the Bible is just an old document and has no relevance for our modern times has obviously never read some of these Proverbs. Notice that King Solomon advises against even talking to a fool, and the reason is that the fool will most likely not want to listen to reason.

So, Abigail has been going to your church for several years. She brings her kids each Sunday and her husband does not come to church. And Abigail comes up to you, a church leader, and she says, "I can't take living with Nabal any longer." She is crying and she says, "He beat me up about four years ago, the police were never called, and since then I live in fear. I just back away whenever he gets so mad that I feel that he is about to hit me." If the battery that occurred is three years old or older, it would not fall under the statute of limitations in most states, so no legal action could be taken. If Nabal is using verbal and emotional abuse against Abigail, but none of it seems to rise to what would be considered Disorderly Conduct, then there may not be (in some states) anything that could be pursued by law enforcement. If you tell her to just go home and be a good wife and mother, she will continue to live in a hazardous environment and the kids will also be forced to stay in a home where fear and intimidation are a part of everyday living.

So, let's suppose you as a priest, pastor or elder decide that you will try to intervene in this problem. Church leaders too often say, "Gee, we have a model of how to go about confronting people, and it was given by Jesus himself in the Book of Matthew Chapter 18 verses 15-17." Which reads: "Moreover if thy brother shall trespass against thee, go tell him his fault between thee and him alone: if he shall hear thee, thou hast gained thy brother. But if he will not hear thee, then take with thee one or two more, that in the mouth of two or three witnesses every word may be established. And if he shall neglect to hear them, tell it unto the church: but if he neglects to hear the church, let him be unto thee as an heathen man and publican," (KJV).

Or, in the NIV, "If your brother sins against you, go and show him his fault, just between the two of you. If he listens to you, you have won your brother over. But if he will not listen, take one or two others along, so that 'every matter may be established by the testimony of two or three witnesses.'" (Jesus was quoting from Deuteronomy 19:15.) "If he refuses to listen to them, tell it to the church; and if he refuses to listen even to the church, treat him as you would a pagan or a tax collector."

The church leader then tells Abigail, "So, you see, you have to go talk to Nabal on your own first. Tell him how much you hate the way he is treating you. If he changes, then you have won him over, if he doesn't, well, then come back and let me know and I can go with another elder, and we'll tell him to knock it off."

The problem here is that Abigail has most likely already told Nabal how she feels, and you are misinterpreting the instruction because this Nabal is not a believer, and he is not a part of the church. Jesus was talking about how to carry out church discipline, and this formula does not apply to this particular Nabal. Jesus' instructions here go hand-in-hand with verses 12-14 of the same chapter when he spoke of the lost sheep. That if one sheep strayed away from the flock, wouldn't you leave the 99 others behind and look for that lost sheep?

So, with this Nabal, forget the church discipline procedure as it does not apply to him. Instead, you need to invite Abigail into your office, make a phone call to the local domestic violence advocacy agency, and have an advocate come in and safety plan with her and the following action needs to be taken: Abigail needs to get extra keys to her car, she needs the birth certificates of the children, she needs copies of credit card statements and other financial information. She needs a safe place to go – such as the shelter that the advocacy agency may provide or, better yet, the home of a church member where she and her kids could stay for a while – a place where Nabal will not know where she is.

Once these things are in place, then you and another elder, pastor or deacon can go meet with Nabal. I would suggest going to his home right about the time he would be coming home from work. Tell him who you are, and tell him that his wife came to you for help because of the abusive relationship and environment that exists in the home. Tell him that she wants to reconcile, but he needs to commit to marriage counseling with her. Tell him that she will call him tonight, but let him know that she will not be using her cell phone, that she will be blocking the call by dialing *67 first, and tell him that the pastoral staff, the elders and the church stand behind her and are willing to do whatever it takes to keep her and the children safe.

Nabal will most likely deny that he has done anything. He may tell you that it isn't that bad, and he will tell you that, "For a Christian, you should see how she behaves." Tell him that a marriage counselor is the best forum for that and reiterate that she is somewhere safe and that she will call him. Nabal will most likely be very irate, he will demand to know where she and the kids are. He may take the church directory and start calling church members asking if they know where she is. He may even drive past the homes of church members to see if her car is parked in anyone's driveway. (It is a good idea to pick a home that has a garage where she can park her car.) Nabal will most likely call the police and threaten to have her arrested for kidnapping. You may want to warn Abigail to not use her cell phone, or to even keep it turned off. Nabal could call their cell phone provider, and if her phone has GPS on it, he may be able to find out where the phone is, or where the phone was when the last call came in.

How this is orchestrated is very crucial. If she leaves on a Friday, she may be off from work until Monday, which would give Nabal a few days to cool down, as he will be at her place of employment on Monday and things will escalate from there. Nabal will probably even show up at the school on Monday to pick up the kids. He has every legal right to do that, and his next step will be to change the locks on the house and refuse her entry to the home. She will likely then call the police, who will tell Nabal that he cannot lock her out. Without a court order regarding the placement of the children, there will likely be nothing that can be done if Abigail decides to try to take the kids back where she was staying. Abigail will then go back home and things will really be tense for her. Violence could escalate, and she will be told that she is no longer allowed to go to church. If Nabal escalates, Abigail needs to dial 9-1-1 immediately. If the police can then arrest Nabal for a domestic violence related offense, Abigail can then sign (in Wisconsin) for the 72 hour no contact to be enforced. This will give her time to contact her advocate and apply for a long-term restraining order. The goal all along is still restoration, but the ball is now in Nabal's court – this is his wake up call. Depending on the nature of the offense (if he is arrested), the court will likely impose a no contact order with the victim as a bond condition. This route is painful, but why should Abigail and the children be uprooted from their home and be on the outside looking in, especially when Nabal is the one who created the current atmosphere and situation?

If Nabal does not blow up, if he sees the errors of his ways and agrees to counseling, he may want to choose the counselor. Abigail may want to insist on a Christian counselor, and church leaders should have a listing of local counselors who are available to meet with them. One huge barrier to counseling is that not everyone has insurance that covers it, and many lack the funds to pay for it on their own. Maybe there is a counselor who attends your church who would intervene for free or at a reduced cost. Perhaps your church and others in your community could join together in paying a counselor to provide services for multiple congregations.

You can see that these interventions not only take time, but they also require money. Few churches budget money to help people with these costs. But if a church is to truly care for people and model the love, concern and grace that Jesus showed, there will be a cost. Some church leaders have a hard time with the thought of helping people with church money. But take a look at the early church from Acts 1:44-47: "All the believers were together and had everything in common. Selling their possessions and goods, they gave to anyone as he had need. Every day they continued to meet together in the temple courts. They broke bread in their homes and ate together with glad and sincere hearts, praising God and enjoying the favor of all the people. And the Lord added to their number daily of those being saved." Can you imagine that, this was the first rummage sale. People selling their things to help someone else. This is the model, that is how the church should respond to the needs of others.

This Nabal will either be won over, or the worst case scenario will be the marriage ending in a divorce. Yes, I did say the "D" word, but remember that this would be the last resort, restoration is the goal all the way through the intervention. We will take a look at divorce in the next chapter.

Now, if this Abigail comes to you and tells you straight out that she was beaten last night, shoved yesterday, sexually assaulted or abused in any way that would be probable cause for law enforcement to make an arrest, you should do the following: Involve an advocate from the local domestic violence agency and encourage Abigail to make a police report. And do not be afraid to let law enforcement meet with her right there at the church. Too many church leaders get too upset about a squad car in the church parking lot. "What will our neighbors think?" they ask, and the answer is who cares. Neighbors will not know why the squad is there and it doesn't matter. After Nabal is arrested, then no contact orders can be put into place. Then the court can order that he receive anger management or some other form of counseling. If Nabal was drinking, he may receive a no drink order imposed by the court as a bond condition. This is Nabal's wake up call, he will either change his ways or let the relationship die, but the ball is in his court. Remember, nothing changes if nothing changes.

Now, church attending Nabal is slightly different. In fact, church going, ministry leading, small group teaching Nabal can be even nastier and harder to deal with than non-believing Nabal. So, this Abigail comes to her pastor, elder or priest and says, "My husband, you won't believe me because you only get to see his nice side, but he really is a terrible man and I live in constant fear of him. He never yells at me, he doesn't hit me, but ten years ago he threw me down the stairs. He did not allow me to go to the hospital and there never was a police report. But now, whenever he wants his way in anything, he calmly looks up from his paper and says, 'Abigail, how would you like to take another trip down the stairs?'" With this Nabal, Jesus' model of church discipline from Matthew 18:15-17 would apply, so let's look at the best way to approach him.

Chances are that Abigail has already gone to him one-on-one and told him that what he did and what he is doing now are wrong. And even if she hasn't, fear of what may happen to her could be a huge deterrent. So, if a church leader says, "Well, you have to go to him first, to tell him how you feel, tell him that you talked to your pastor and tell him that he needs to change," in most cases if she tells her husband that she talked to the pastor this Nabal will lash out at her for saying anything to anyone. He will demand to know what she told and how many others know. This Nabal will go into damage control mode. He will call the pastor to deny the allegations, and he will likely threaten Abigail and tell her to recant what she said. Her safety is in jeopardy, and if she refuses to recant, he may escalate and hurt her even more. If the church leaders continue to ask questions and make inquiries, this Nabal will likely withdraw his and his family's memberships at the church. He will go find a new church somewhere where no one knows the big secret. If Abigail refuses to leave the church with him, she is placed in extreme danger of increased violence.

The best way to intervene is to set up a meeting with Abigail and an advocate from your local domestic violence advocacy agency. Her protection is the most important consideration throughout the process. In fact, I am convinced that a phone call to the local advocacy agency is more important than a call to 9-1-1. The arrest itself is an important component, but if there is no safety planning, when Nabal is released from jail – and he will eventually be released – Abigail's well being and the safety of the children are at great risk.

Abigail should be somewhere safe – either at a shelter or in the home of a church member, and the pastor and an elder could go meet with Nabal. I know that Jesus recommends one person for the first encounter, but we are talking about a potentially dangerous person and it may not be safe for just one to go.

Once Abigail is safe, you go meet with Nabal. You tell him that you care about his family and that you learned from Abigail that there was a serious physical altercation ten years ago, but while it doesn't appear that any laws are being violated now, he is violating God's laws in terms of how husbands should treat their wives. You could share with him these passages:

1 Corinthians 13:1-8 (NIV): "And now I will show you the most excellent way. If I speak in the tongues of men and angels, but have

not love, I am only a resounding gong or a clanging cymbal. If I have the gift of prophesy and can fathom all mysteries and all knowledge, and if I have a faith that can move mountains, but have not love, I am nothing. If I give all that I possess to the poor and surrender my body to the flames, but have not love, I gain nothing. Love is patient, love is kind. It does not envy, it does not boast, it is not proud. It is not rude, it is not self-seeking, it is not easily angered, it keeps no record of wrongs. Love does not delight in evil but rejoices with the truth. It always protects, always trusts, always hopes, always perseveres." (And chances are that he read this aloud or heard it read on the day that he was married.)

Genesis 2:24: "For this reason a man will leave his father and mother and be united with his wife, and they will become one flesh," (NIV). This was most likely also read at his wedding, and never implied that Nabal should no longer care for his parents, but signaled a joining with his wife, in God's institution of marriage, and a new responsibility to care for his wife. It is this idea of two people coming together and forming a oneness. It goes along with Paul's teaching in Ephesians 5:25-30 which reads: "Husbands, love your wives, just as Christ loved the church and gave himself up for her to make her holy, cleansing her by the washing with water through the word, and to present her to himself as a radiant church, without stain or wrinkle or any other blemish, but holy and blameless. In this same way, husbands ought to love their wives as their own bodies. He who loves his wife loves himself. After all, no one ever hated his own body, but he feeds and cares for it, just as Christ does the church – for we are members of his body."

You could remind Nabal that Romans 12:9-10 tells us that, "Love must be sincere. Hate what is evil; cling to what is good. Be devoted to one another in brotherly love. Honor one another above yourselves," (NIV).

If Nabal says, "Yes, I smacked her, but she just knows how to push my buttons," tell him that this is why the Apostle Paul wrote in Romans 12:18, "If it is possible, as far as it depends on you, live at peace with everyone." It is this idea that, since we cannot predict how the other person will treat us, as far as it depends on me, I will live at peace with everyone.

And if Nabal shows or comes out and says that he hates his wife, you can remind him that we read in 1 Peter 3:7, "Husbands, in the same way be considerate as you live with your wives, and treat them with respect as the weaker partner and as heirs with you of the gracious gift of life, so that nothing will hinder your prayers," (NIV). Nabal will come right out and tell you that his wife must submit, and he will have the verses memorized for you. But Peter is saying that submission is also the duty of the husband, not to his wife, but to the duty he has as a husband to care for his wife, being aware of her concerns and fears, along with her feelings and to give up his needs and desires for hers. It is this idea of being the knight in shining armor to come along side of his wife to protect, provide and care for her. And isn't that what Christ did for the church? He gave up his life on the cross for the salvation of his bride – the church. And Peter warns here that there is a barrier in a husband's prayer life if he should not follow these instructions.

Peter says in the same chapter, verse 8 and 9: "Finally, all of you, live in harmony with one another; be sympathetic, love as brothers, be compassionate and humble. Do not repay evil with evil or insult with insult, but with blessing, because to this you were called so that you would inherit a blessing," (NIV).

If you win Nabal over, if he sees the errors in his ways of how he is treating Abigail, if he agrees to go to Christian counseling, then your intervention has been a success, and full restoration of that marriage should be the end result.

In most cases though, the intervention will not go this smoothly. What will likely happen is that Nabal will challenge you, he will be angry, he will tell you that none of this is your business, and he will quote scriptures that he says validates what he is doing.

I was listening to Dr. John McArthur of the radio program "Grace to You" one day, and he was talking about interpreting scriptures the proper way, and the basic idea of his teaching that day was how so many people can find a verse, take it out of context, and make it apply to what they believe. He told a story about a pastor who had noticed that a woman in the congregation had not been in church for several Sundays, so he decided to pay her a visit at her home. The pastor stood on her front porch, and while he was knocking on the door he could hear someone moving around inside of the home. He thought he saw the woman peeking out through a window, but she never answered the door. The pastor then wrote on the back of his business card, "Revelation 3:20 Here I am! I stand at the door and knock. If anyone hears my voice and opens the door, I will come in and eat with him and he with me." The pastor left the card in her mailbox and left. The next Sunday, the woman was in church and she even sat in the front row. After the sermon, on her way out, she handed him a card. On it she had written: "Genesis 3:10b I was afraid because I was naked; so I hid."

Well, Nabal will also have verses for you. I have a friend who works for the court system, and he runs anger management type classes for men in jail who have been sentenced in a domestic violence related incident. Many are incarcerated for six to nine months, and they have been ordered by the court to attend these weekly classes. One day my friend told me that his classes usually run ten weeks or longer, and in a group of ten to fifteen men there is usually one or two who claim to be Christians and they defy every aspect of the training that he provides. He also said that many of them walk in with the following Bible verses written down, and they challenge his instruction and ask him to explain why they should learn about anger management when the Bible gives them the privilege to do what they were doing. Here are the top three verses brought to him:

1 Corinthians 11:5 and 6: "And every woman who prays or prophesies with her head uncovered dishonors her head – it is just as though her head were shaved. If a woman does not cover her head, she should have her hair cut off; and it is a disgrace for a woman to have her

hair cut or shaved off, she should cover her head," (NIV). Well, this verse has to be taken in the context of verse 4 which precedes it which reads: "Every man who prays or prophesies with his head covered dishonors his head," (NIV). In Corinth at the time of Paul's writing, there was probably a local custom that men wore head coverings. We know that some Jews did in New Testament times, and many more Jews did so in the fourth century A.D. Men in Corinth were wearing head coverings and Paul was telling them that it was not proper. Not that it was a command of God, but that in that society, at that time, an uncovered head of a man was an outward sign of his authority over women and women were to have their heads covered.

Paul was saying, according to their local customs, that for a man to cover his head the same way that women did was contrary to their roles. So, in verse 5 where Paul speaks about women, he was stating that women were not to lead or speak in church. Women could pray, they could teach other women and children, but they were not to teach or lead men. But this has to be looked at in terms of how women were viewed in the era of Paul. Women had no rights, they were treated as property and, even today, there are countries in the Middle East where women must wear a veil and have their bodies totally covered. There are countries today where women have no voting rights, and some countries still prohibit women from being able to drive a car.

It is interesting to note that the Bible tells us that Timothy received his biblical teaching from his mother and grandmother, so we can see that women do have great value as teachers, it was just prohibited at the local church towards men. The requirement that they do pray with their heads covered goes back again to their local customs and to show a proper distinction between men and women.

So, I really do not see why jail inmates bring these verses with them to their batterers' treatment group as proof that they were wrongly convicted or that the anger management material does not apply to them. Nowhere in these verses does Paul say that a man or a woman has the right to abuse his or her spouse.

The next verse that showed up frequently at his treatment groups was Colossians 3:18, "Wives submit to your husbands, as is fitting in the Lord." (Other men also had Ephesians 5:22 which basically says the same thing.) The important thing to look at about submission is that everyone must submit to someone. And while submitting, the person doing the submission is never told that they must submit. They are not constantly reminded that they must submit, they just submit to please the Lord. The Greek verb submit means to subject oneself, which gives this idea of someone placing themselves under another of their own free will. And while some men keep reminding their wife that they must submit, isn't it interesting that men must also submit? 1 Peter 5:5 instructs, "Young men in the same way be submissive to those who are older. Clothe yourselves with humility toward one another, because, 'God opposes the proud but gives grace to the humble,'" (NIV). Romans 13:1 and 2 reads: "Everyone must submit himself to the governing authorities, for there is no authority except that which God has established. The authorities that exist have been established by God. Consequently, he who rebels against the authority is rebelling against what God has instituted, and those who do so will bring judgment on themselves," (NIV).

So, if a man or woman is abusing his or her spouse, not only are they violating the laws of God in terms of how they are to treat others, but they are also violating the laws of man, and Paul is telling us that earthly laws are to be followed since governments and rulers were established by God. The only exception to this command would be if ruling bodies required that man do something that was contrary to God's word. Men must also, according to James 4:7, "Submit yourselves to God . . ." (NIV), and you have to ask a Nabal who brings up the whole submission argument, how can you submit to God, accept God's gift of salvation, be humble and still abuse your wife, and try to excuse the abuse as merely making sure that your wife is submitting to you?

We read in 1 Peter 2:18, "Slaves, submit yourselves to your masters with all respect, not only to those who are good and considerate, but also to those who are harsh," (NIV). Well, we do not think of ourselves as slaves, but this slave/master relationship applies to any superior that we may have. The modern day example would be an employee/employer relationship in which we as workers submit to our bosses every day. And, isn't it interesting that unless you have a bullying boss, our bosses do not run around all day, every day, telling us, "Now remember, you must submit!" or, "You better submit to me or else!" In fact, nowhere in the Bible do we read that the person doing the submission is ever reminded or bullied into submitting. In fact, at work, we go in, we do our job and our employer pays us each week. And, in most cases, even our employer has to submit to someone or even a board of directors.

The church is told to submit to Christ in Ephesians 5:24, and Christ himself submitted to the will of God the Father as we read in Matthew 26:39 when Jesus went to pray in the Garden of Gethsemane just prior to his arrest. "Going a little farther, he fell with his face to the ground and prayed, 'My Father, if it is possible, may this cup be taken from me. Yet not as I will, but as you will,'" (NIV). Several years back I was teaching a teenage Sunday school class and we read this passage. One of the kids in the class asked me if this meant that Jesus was looking for a way out of having to die on the cross. I told the class that Jesus had never been separated from God the Father, and he knew that between the time of his death and his resurrection that there would be this separation. The other thing to consider is that the word "cup" is an Old Testament reference as a symbol of divine wrath. Jesus knew that he would bear the sins of all – past, present and future – and his cries to have the cup pass him shows just how awful the cup of wrath was going to be. But, still, he submitted himself to the will of the Father, and did you notice that God never yelled down to Jesus, "YOU BETTER SUBMIT!!" or, "COME ON NOW, YOU HAVE TO DO WHAT I SAY!!" But that is exactly how some men try to get their wives to submit, by constantly throwing into their faces passages that deal with submission.

I arrested a guy one time for battering his wife, and on the way to jail he said to me, "You obviously don't go to church or you would know that she must submit to me in every way." I asked him what that meant, and he said that it means he has the final word in all decisions. "Is that so?" I asked. "Yes!" he replied. I suggested then that after he is bonded out of jail, that tomorrow he should go to the nearest car dealership and buy a brand new car without his wife present. "Well, gee, I couldn't do that." "Why not?" I asked. "Well, my wife would want some say in the color, or the model. It wouldn't be such a great idea. Plus, she would also have to be there to sign for the loan." I asked him then if he really is the final say in everything, and he conceded that maybe there are some things that he could not make her submit to.

The only instance where I can see that maybe the husband could make a final decision would be in the following circumstance: Let's say a guy was called into his boss's office, and the manager told him that his company was closing its office here and he had two options. He could take a severance package and lose his job, or he and his family could relocate 950 miles away from here and take a similar position in another office of the company. The boss gives him two weeks to make up his mind. This guy goes home and tells his wife and she flat out refuses to move away from here. After all, all of their family and friends live here. So, the husband searches the classifieds, posts his resume with numerous other companies, and he just can't find any job that would pay remotely close to what he is making now. The boss needs his answer the next day and, considering the lost wages, considering the loss of health insurance, and considering the future loss of his retirement package, he tells his wife we are moving, I have to take this job. Submission of a wife to a husband does not involve just minuscule, trivial, day-to-day decisions. These should always be discussed and figured out together as one flesh would cooperate and compliment another. All submission means is that in the rare, really huge decisions that come along, the husband holds the trump card and makes an important decision that needs to be made. And, this example is the only thing I can come up with to show as an example of what that decision would be.

Men, or even church leaders, who would say that submission allows a husband to physically, verbally, emotionally, sexually or in any other way abuse his wife are flat out wrong and have disregarded all of the Bible's instructions on how Christians are supposed to love and care for one another. And, chances are that if a husband is truly loving his wife and caring for her the way that Christ loved the church, I'll show you a wife who would have no qualms about following that lead or submitting to a husband like that.

So, after you have shared the verses that deal with how a husband should care for his wife, and if you do not run into a big debate about submission, and if this Nabal says that, yes, he has been harsh and agrees to go to counseling, then you have won him over.

But, if Nabal stonewalls and denies that there is even a problem, then his wife is still going to have to remain somewhere safe. The problem now becomes, how long can Abigail stay away and safe while we wait for Nabal to come to his senses and move towards restoration of the marriage? He will try to get the kids while they are in school, he will still show up at church, sit behind her and scowl at her or approach her in a violent manner. Nabal will usually withhold funds from Abigail, and unless she has her own job, he will hold out and wait for her to come back due to the lack of money. At some point, Abigail will be forced to file for a legal separation or a divorce in order for child custody/visitation issues and child support and other financial issues to be dealt with. Nabals who are difficult to deal with will need a court order to convince them that they must fulfill their legal, financial and parental obligations. And, just because a divorce or legal separation is filed, does not mean that the marriage cannot still be restored. Remember, this is Nabal's wake up call. The fact that he has been served with divorce papers may be what he needs to change.

I know people who have reconciled a month before their final divorce hearing. I know of couples who have dropped the whole divorce case at the final hearing, and still others have re-married after a divorce. The men involved in these cases have even told me that it wasn't until they were served did they realize what they had been doing wrong and just how serious their wife was about bringing about a change in the way that she was being treated.

The whole process of a temporary order to deal with child custody and financial issues can be a long and very difficult process. More women have been severely injured or killed right after their husbands were served with either a temporary restraining order or divorce papers. Don't think that you can predict how a husband will respond to being served. Church leaders are sometimes fooled by abusers into believing that they will remain clam and non-violent towards their spouses. Remember, the best predictor of future behavior is past behavior, and if that past behavior has been violent, then future behavior, especially after being served with legal action, has a very high potential of being violent.

It may come to the point where the church leaders will have to go to the congregation and tell them what has happened and to announce that this church member has been asked not to attend church here anymore. This is a last resort and, again, restoration is the goal. Remember, he is that lost sheep that has strayed from the flock, and in following church discipline, as outlined by Jesus, church leaders need to make every attempt to find and restore that lost sheep.

The problem too often in churches today is that churches do not want to follow church discipline procedures. People just continue going to church pretending that there isn't this problem between this couple. Abigail will say, and rightfully so, why should I leave my church home? I did nothing wrong, it was him. And Nabal will continue to show up and say that he refuses to leave the church, and he will even try to continue leading in his church ministry. Church leaders need to tell him that he cannot continue to teach a class or sing in the choir or serve on the finance team while all of this unresolved conflict is going on in his life and marriage.

Oftentimes I have seen men who were separated from their wives, yet still show up at the same church each Sunday, being rude to their wife and even partaking in communion. Such a man should be told that he cannot take communion while he is refusing to restore his own marriage. Paul tells us in 1 Corinthians 11:27-29: "Therefore, whoever eats the bread or drinks the cup of the Lord in an unworthy manner will be guilty of sinning against the body and blood of the Lord. A man ought to examine himself before he eats of the bread and drinks of the cup. For anyone who eats and drinks without recognizing the body of the Lord eats and drinks judgment on himself," (NIV). This "unworthy manner" would apply to such a Nabal because he is bitter, has an ungodly reaction to his wife and is unrepentant.

During the restoration process, it is not uncommon that a Christian counselor or a church leader, trying to act as a mentor, will meet with Nabal and the meetings turn into a waste of time. There are men who have been meeting with a church leader for one-on-one help, for four years or more, and there has been absolutely no change whatsoever in Nabal's attitude towards his wife. One day, Nabal is going back to his wife to ask forgiveness, then the next time they meet, Nabal is back hurling insults at his wife and refusing to make any changes in how he deals with her. And, the common mistake that peer helpers make is not calling Nabal on it and saying that his actions and his heart do not match up to how a Christian is supposed to react and behave. There comes a point during these interventions when it becomes clear that Nabal refuses to acknowledge his wrong, and refuses to work towards restoring his marriage, that the counselor or the peer helper needs to come right out and tell Nabal that the meetings are done, that the time spent is futile due to his unwillingness to take responsibility for his actions. That the hatred and resentment that he harbors against his wife are unacceptable, and the person trying to help needs to back off and quit meeting with him. Remind Nabal that Jesus told us that the fruit we bear will tell the world what is going on inside of us, and that there is no evidence of Christian love or humility, and until there is you no longer wish to meet with or mentor him.

Now, some may say that this is being judgmental and that the Bible says in Matthew 7:1: "Do not judge, or you too will be judged," (NIV). Jesus was warning about a self-righteous, legalistic judgment which was being exercised by the Pharisees. This does not prevent all types of judging as churches are to carry out wise discernment, and we are not talking about unfair judgment. We are talking about calling sin – sin and it is part of the restoration process. John 7:24 reads, "Stop judging by mere appearances, and make a right judgment," (NIV). And the same verse in the New King James Version reads: "Do not judge according to appearance, but judge with righteous judgment." Jesus here again was warning against a legalistic judgment, but allowed theological discernment in a correct and Biblical way. So we do have the right to call Nabal on his behavior and to tell him that he is wrong.

When you meet with Nabal in an effort to intervene, be prepared for one-way conversations. Nabal will try to do all the talking, he will minimize his behavior, and he will try to get you to agree with him and collude with him. Nabal will word his questions to you in such a way that you must respond with a "yes," almost as though it will sound like you are agreeing with him. He will ask you, "So, you are telling me that you have never argued with your wife?" Or, he will ask you, "Don't you believe that the Bible says that the wife must submit?' And the proper thing to do is to remind him that this is about him, not you, and that you are not going to let him control and dominate the conversation. A Nabal is very controlling by nature, that is why he is in the dilemma that he is in. Do not allow him to control your conversation, and when you notice that he is trying to, cut him off right away and direct the focus of the meeting back to him and his behaviors.

Nabal will tell you that he has been praying about his marital situation, and that God has shown him that he is correct. Consider this story: Nabal and Abigail have been married for 13 years and they have two daughters, 8 and 4. Abigail grew up in church and her dad is an elder. Nabal also grew up in church and he leads two ministries. What people at church do not know is that Nabal is very harsh towards his wife, and the home environment is very hostile. It wasn't that way while Abigail was dating him. It started shortly after the two married. He told her right away, "I wear the pants in this house." He belittles his wife, criticizes her constantly. He makes all the decisions and she feels helpless and worthless. After years of this treatment, she does what any other person would do. She decides to stand up for herself because she has been downgraded for so long that she feels backed into a corner. Verbal arguments escalate to physical altercations. Lately, even their girls have tried to get into the middle of the pushing, shoving and shouting matches. Things are tense at home all of the time. But at church Nabal covers it all up and acts very nice and polite to everyone and makes everyone think that he has the perfect marriage and home life.

Until one day Nabal goes to Abigail and says, "Something has got to change. You were very obedient to me for many years and now you are rebelling." He goes on to say, "I have been praying about what to do, and I feel God telling me to go on a two week vacation – alone, so that I can clear my head and pray about what to do next. When I return, one of two things will happen. We will either stay together and you start shaping up and obeying me again, or you will move out and I will stay here with the kids. You can either move back with your parents, or maybe your sister will take you in."

Nabal goes on his vacation and only calls home twice during the entire two weeks. In the last phone call, he hints to Abigail that the response he has gotten from God, from his hours of prayer, is that when he returns she will have to move out. Instead of waiting around to see what he will say, she files for a temporary order of protection, and she visits an attorney and has papers drawn up to initiate a divorce. When Nabal returns, he is quickly served with both documents and he finds himself staying at a friend's house. Nabal is very angry, he is angry that his wife delivered a preemptive first strike, thus ruining his chances of being the boss, being in control and being the one to call the shots.

Now, let's stop here for a moment. Some church leaders trying to intervene will have a hard time telling Nabal that there is no way that God was the one telling him that he should go on vacation alone, and that God could not have been the one telling him that he should kick his wife out of the house. We know this because that would be totally contrary to what the Bible instructs about unconditional love, rules for Christian living and how a husband should love and care for his wife.

Now, if Abigail, who is married to church going Nabal tells her pastor, priest or elder that she was shoved, pushed, slapped, punched, held against her will or anything else that would constitute a crime, this action should be taken: First, an advocate from the local domestic violence agency should be brought in to meet with Abigail and a plan made for her safety and the safety of their children. And, while we never want to be telling Abigail what she should or should not do, she should be strongly encouraged to make a report with the local law enforcement agency and Nabal should be arrested. Now, I know that many people in church wonder if an arrest is the proper way to treat a "fellow believer," but we have to ask ourselves again, would a "fellow believer" be treating his wife in such a cruel way and could he really be a "fellow believer?" Remember, an arrest is Nabal's wake up call. The arrest itself could be the impetus for him to change his behavior. Remember, too, that restoration is still the goal. Most victims of domestic violence that I have dealt with rarely want a divorce. They recall many other happy times in the marriage – they just want the abuse to end.

And if you think that an arrest is non-biblical, look at what Paul wrote in Romans 13 verses 2-7 (New King James Version): "Therefore whoever resists authority resists the ordinance of God, and those who resist will bring judgment on themselves. For rulers are not a terror to good works, but to evil. Do you want to be unafraid of the authority? Do what is good, and you will have praise from the same. For he is God's minister to you for good. But if you do evil, be afraid; for he does not bear the sword in vain; for he is God's minister, an avenger to execute wrath on him who practices evil. Therefore, you must be subject, not only because of wrath but also for conscience' sake. For because of this you pay taxes, for they are God's ministers attending continually to this very thing. Render therefore to all their due: taxes to whom taxes are due, customs to whom customs, fear to whom fear, honor to whom honor." Here again, we have Paul telling us that government and civil laws are still God's doing, even though they are earthly laws made by men. He wasn't talking about God's wrath, but of the wrath that government can have on people who disobey laws and do evil. The one who bears the sword here are the men and women of law enforcement and the men and women who are prosecutors and judges, enforcing and carrying out the laws that were created by elected representatives and signed by governors or presidents.

So, if Nabal is arrested, and if there is no contact order enforced by the courts, Abigail will most likely not feel the need to go to a shelter or move in with someone from church. Abigail will be able to stay in the home, and hopefully Nabal will be humbled and broken by being temporarily removed from his home. This will be his wake up call. If convicted for domestic violence offense(s), the court will most likely order that he attend anger management or a batterer's treatment group. This, too, will be a wake up call, and hopefully he will learn and see how wrong he has been.

After his release from jail, you as the church leader can go meet with him in the hopes of getting him to agree to go to a Christian counselor. Restoration of the marriage is still the ultimate goal, and there are many cases where a repentant, contrite Nabal has emerged as a wonderful, caring, loving husband and father.

But don't be too surprised if he remains defiant and fights the charges tooth and nail and refuses to accept responsibility. Offenders need to be held accountable, and if they have committed a crime, the court system is the perfect place for that accountability to begin. Abigail may still end up needing to file for a legal separation or divorce. Again, child custody/ visitation issues and financial issues and obligations need to be addressed, and if you think Nabal will just make things smooth and easy, watch out, because in most cases they are angry and not willing to listen to reason.

If Nabal is an elder or pastor, and he has committed an act of domestic violence which rises to the level where a crime has been committed, he, too, should be arrested. During the time that he is out on bond, and until the case is adjudicated, he should be made to step down from his position within the church. If he pleads guilty or is convicted by a jury, he should not be restored to a church leadership position or to a church pastorate until sufficient time has passed and it is clear to all, especially Abigail, that there has been change.

Some people in the church argue that an elder cannot be arrested because in 1 Timothy 5:19, Paul wrote: "Do not entertain an accusation against an elder unless it is brought by two or three witnesses," (NIV). Paul was talking about frivolous complaints brought on by members of the church or evil people, making up things to discredit an elder. Just because one wife comes forward to tell the pastor that her husband, who is an elder, has abused her, does not mean that the pastor should not proceed with any action because there is only one accuser – the elder's wife. Chances are that there are several or many other witnesses. The children in the home may have witnessed the abuse. A neighbor may have heard or seen something. There could be disclosure witnesses – people whom the victim reported the crime to right after it happened. The church is not an investigative authority, the police or sheriff's department in your community is. Just because the abuser is an elder, that does not mean that the church should fail to act, fail to protect, or fail to move forward and assist the victim.

Many churches often coddle abusers in the church. Many church leaders who are trying to make an intervention into the lives of an abuser and the victim spend months, even years trying to convince Nabal that he needs to change. There is nothing wrong with that because, after all, restoration is the ultimate goal. But there does come a point when Nabal needs to be told that unless he repents and changes, you are done meeting with him and listening to his excuses and minimizations.

I listen to a radio program, "Proclaim," on my car radio every morning on my way home from work. This program is a twenty minute daily teaching by Dr. Michael Easley who is the President of The Moody Bible Institute in Chicago, Illinois. On December 4, 2007, his teaching was part 2 of a message entitled "Fighting the Good Fight," and here is a quote from that broadcast, just in case you are thinking that it is wrong to back away from Nabal when he refuses wise counsel month after month, year after year. This portion of his teaching dealt with excommunication in the church, and he made it very clear that restoration is always the ultimate goal, however. "It is and I think a lot of churches historically have done this wrong, they've done it improperly. In our text today we are going to see where Paul talks about two people that are shipwrecked in regard to their faith, and so it opens up this discussion of when a person sins, what are the consequences ultimately? And this is sort of the sad ending of a person who continues, who persists in sin. It's a hard example, it's an extreme example Paul uses but he prays that he delivers them over to Satan. And, of course, some of you have studied this and you probably know a whole lot more about it than I do. There are a number of tandem passages that we can look at to sort of see Paul's meaning. The bottom line is some sort of think it's an excommunication; they've been set apart. There are all sorts of nuances and degrees of excommunication it may or not be. If it fits in the Context of 1st Corinthians 5:5 where Paul hands a person over for destruction, that sort of turns up the heat on the story just a little bit. There is a time when a person so turns against God and the things of God that Paul says that 'I've delivered them over to Satan.' Now, there are layers of this. We don't have time to discuss them, but number one, the goal first and always is restoration, not getting even or retaliation. Do you remember Jesus corrects the disciples for an attitude of retribution? Remember? So, you want to be careful when and if you get into these kinds of experiences. Listen to 1st Thessalonians 3:14-15; 'If anyone does not obey your instruction in this letter, take special note of that person that he may be put to shame, yet do not regard him as an enemy but admonish him as a brother.' The immediate goal when a person goes off into sin is not to punish them or bring retribution or turn them over to Satan. The immediate goal is found in Galatians 6:1-2. The immediate goal is to restore such a one to bring them back to restoration. But there is a time from the passage in 1ˢᵗ Corinthians 5:5 where Paul says, 'Enough.' And you have to be very careful when you come to that. That's sort of my lesson here. I have on occasions prayed that God would make a sinner miserable. I have on a number of occasions prayed that prayer. When a person has resisted counsel again and again, when they have said 'no' to this thing and you've come along side and they've left their wife, left their family, left their kids, you say, 'Look . . .' and you try and knock some sense into them. And there's a period of time when you're wasting your time.

"I remember one individual that I worked with for a lot of breakfasts trying to encourage this person to go back to his wife and family. It was going nowhere. My thumbnail was I'll work with them as long as they're equivocating. You can come up with a better one. But if one day they're going to leave, one day they're going to stay, one day they feel guilty, one day they don't, I'll try to stay in the fight with them. But when they finally go, 'I'm out of here no matter what you do,' then I say, 'You know what? I've got other things to do. I'll pray you're miserable.' I tell them that to their face. I'll leave them voice mails: 'I'm praying you're miserable today.' I'll send them an e-mail: 'I hope you're enjoying your misery. I hope God will crush you until you come back to Him.' Now, I've never gone to the last part to say, 'God kill them,' and that's what Paul does in 1ˢᵗ Corinthians 5:5. 'God, the damage they're doing to the body of Christ is so huge, it'd be better if You'd take them now and end the consequence of their destruction of their sin in other people's lives. Take them out Lord.' Now, I've wanted to pray that prayer but I have never prayed it. I have prayed that God would make them absolutely miserable in their choice to walk away from Him. I think it's a good prayer. When it gets tough, when it gets hard, when it gets difficult, keep your commission. Don't forget the benchmark; why you did this thing. Go back to the beginning place where you started. Keep a good conscience."

Chapter Six

Helping Abigail

TOO MANY TIMES, THOSE PEOPLE who try to help victims of domestic violence fail to understand the seriousness of the situation. Churches especially try to tell Abigail that even Jesus had to suffer, and they tell victims that there is great reward in just keeping silent and persevering. My favorite is when people tell victims, "Well you know, Romans 8:28 says: 'And we know that in all things God works for the good of those who love him, who have been called according to his purpose.'" Not very comforting words for Abigail when her daily life is a constant barrage of insults. Not very comforting for someone who is walking on eggshells, not knowing what will trigger the abuser into an escalation of the violence. Most victims will tell you that they cannot sleep, and even in cases where the abuse is not physical, the effects are. They can't eat, they often have constant headaches, are plagued by ulcers, they suffer anxiety attacks. They feel as though they are withering away. The constant punishment of screaming, yelling, the threats and the mind games are just too much for anyone to bear. Most victims will tell you that they just cannot go on living in the home environment that is more dangerous to them than the crime and violence in the outside world.

Many victims of intimate partner violence will tell you that their abuser acts like a king. It's amazing, too, the number of child witnesses to violence at home who will tell me, "My dad acts like he is a king, he's always demanding things of my mom and me." I find it interesting that so many victims and children describe the abuser as a king, or one that acts like a king. Do you recall in the very first chapter of this book, in the account of Abigail and Nabal, from 1 Samuel Chapter 25, that after Abigail returned from meeting David, she found Nabal: "He was in the house holding a banquet like that of a king." Interesting that Nabal's come across to their family members as someone who has lots of authority, someone who acts like a king.

I spoke to several women victims of domestic violence and asked them what their church had done to either help them or hinder them. Here are some examples and some feedback so that you can get a better idea of what good interventions look like, and what bad interventions look like.

Abigail and Nabal have been married for 18 years. They have a 13 year old son and an 8 year old daughter. Abigail fell in love with Nabal because he was so caring and loving towards her. They went to church together and he seemed like the perfect person to marry. But, after the wedding, Nabal refused to go to church with her. He quit paying any bills and kept his salary for himself. Had it not been for the fact that Abigail had a good paying, full-time job, they would have lost their home and their cars many years ago. Abigail has been constantly cut down, yelled at, sworn at, and while there was some shoving and slapping years ago, recently Nabal has stepped up with the physical assaults. Abigail finds herself wearing long sleeved blouses to work, even on the hottest days in summer, just to cover the bruises, scratch marks and even bite marks on her arms. No one knows what she is going through. She is too embarrassed to say anything to anyone.

Nabal runs a restaurant and has had affairs in the past. He is constantly flirting with all of the new waitresses that he hires and he goes to the local strip club almost every night. Abigail has asked him over and over again to come to church with her and Nabal refuses. One day, Abigail says to herself, I am tired of living like this. I would be better off on my own since I already rely on my own money and I can't stand the awful treatment that I am subjected to. So, one day she tells Nabal that she is going to get an attorney and get a divorce. Nabal laughs at her and tells her that she will never see one dime in child support. She asks him to go to counseling and he angrily tells her, "I don't need a counselor."

Abigail goes to church one Sunday and tells her close friend what has been going on and that she is filing for a divorce. This friend does everything that she can to dissuade Abigail from calling the attorney. Well, Abigail does it anyway and, after he is served, Nabal becomes very upset and the verbal and physical abuse become even worse than before.

Now, because this Nabal has a restaurant, just about every ministry in the church calls him to provide meals for the various meetings that they have. And when Nabal delivers the goods, guess what, he never accepts any money for the food, or he provides it for a very nominal fee. Abigail has asked the various ministry leaders to please get their food from a different caterer. She explains that every time she goes to court for the proceedings, which are for the purposes of determining child support and even placement of the children, Nabal's attorney keeps showing the judge all of the "thank you" notes that Nabal has received from the church for his "generous" donations.

One day, Abigail tells the pastor and an elder that she really is tired of Nabal treating her so poorly, and then using the church donations as bargaining chips in the courtroom. The pastor and elder tell her that since she is a member and attends regularly, that they will try to get the word out – that Nabal should no longer be asked to provide food. But that very next Saturday, the Women's Group at church had a prayer breakfast, and with Abigail seated right at the front of the room, she is shocked to see Nabal walking in with trays of food. Abigail talks to the leader of the women's breakfast group and asks her if the church leadership had asked the ministry leaders to quit relying on her husband to provide food. The response: "Yes, they did ask that, but our budget is tight and we decided to call him anyway. He is such a wonderful person and he is such a great cook." Abigail is very hurt and goes back to the pastor. He tells her that she is just being difficult, and that one way to win him over is for him to continue to have contact with the church. Abigail is in tears and says, "You know and I know, that except for a couple Easter and Christmas Eve services he hasn't stepped foot in this place since the day we got married!" She again pleads with the pastors and elders to not call on her husband anymore.

Abigail does not feel supported, and several people in church have told her, "You need to remember the vows that you took, right here in front of God and everybody." Abigail does remember the vows that she took, and she wants to fulfill them, but her safety and the safety of her children are on the line. Church leaders need to stop asking the victims to remember their vows, and the focus of that discussion needs to be shifted to Nabal. Chances are that when those vows were taken, Abigail felt loved and cared for, and the manipulation and controlling behaviors of Nabal did not surface until after the marriage. Nabal needs to be reminded, not Abigail, that he promised to "love, honor and cherish" his wife. Is Nabal fulfilling the vows that he made? It is too easy to ask her if she remembers saying, "for better or for worse," and church people too often say, "Well, this must be the worse." After all that we have learned about the risk of great bodily harm or even death, is it really practical to just tell Abigail that this is the "worse" part that she pledged to endure?

Another Abigail also met her husband and both attended church prior to their marriage, and her Nabal quit going. He became very possessive of her, he demanded to know where she was and who she was with all of the time. They have a three year old daughter, and just recently he has begun to shove and push his wife. Abigail is very fearful for her safety and tells Nabal that she wants him to go to marriage counseling. She has the name of a Christian counselor, but he refuses, saying that his insurance will not cover any agency outside of his healthcare plan, and so they go to a counselor provided by his employer. Nabal is a career military supervisor and, at the very first session, he denies any wrong behavior and doesn't even admit to shoving his wife. When the two leave, the counselor tells them both to try to get along, and Abigail is told to call the counselor during business hours if any further physical acts take place. A call to the counselor is preferred rather than a call to the police department.

Two nights later Nabal is shouting and yelling at Abigail, he is escalating, and she thinks it best to take her daughter with her and spend the night at her mom's house. Nabal refuses to let her leave with their child and Abigail tries to call the police, but Nabal grabs the phone and shoves her down to the floor. Later, after Nabal falls asleep, Abigail calls the police department. She does not mention the physical act, but she asks what her rights are with regard to their daughter. She asks if she can just leave with her daughter. The police tell her that she can, however since there has been no legal action and no court order regarding placement, that eventually she will have to return with her daughter.

Abigail stays the night and calls the counselor the next day. The counselor calls them both in, and since the counseling agency is also part of the military, a referral is made to Nabal's commanding officer. Three weeks later there is a military hearing and Abigail gives her testimony regarding the events of that night and is whisked out of the hearing room. Nabal is inside, telling his version of the events to the military panel. After his testimony, Abigail is brought back in to hear the rendering of the decision. The panel found "clear and convincing evidence to determine that this military official was guilty of an act of domestic violence on the night in question." Abigail was then whisked out of the room again for the punishment phase of the hearing. Fifteen minutes later, an angry Nabal emerges from the room, and he refuses to tell her what the determination was. The panel also tells her that they cannot discuss the punishment that was handed down. Abigail later learned from a fellow co-worker of her husband that Nabal had been ordered to turn in his key to the armory. What do you suppose this decision says about Nabal's lethality risk to Abigail? And, why do you think no police report was made? I think that it was handled inside because a domestic violence conviction handed down from the circuit court would mean that Nabal could never again possess a weapon.

After the hearing, things at home are very tense. There are still some violent acts, however Abigail feels too afraid to make the military aware. Some friends at church ask her, "Why would you stay with this guy?" Some ask her, "How many times are you going to be hit before you come to your senses and leave?" These are terrible questions to ask any victim of domestic violence. Most victims are already aware that they are in danger, and most have a plan, but money and other issues usually hamper any escape.

But this Abigail did have a plan. She knew that in three months Nabal had to go to mandatory, two week long military training in California. Abigail secretly lined up a new apartment and had a moving truck rental set up. The very morning that Nabal left, she brought in the truck and started packing. Some of her friends from church helped her and were very supportive. Some friends at church refused and told her that it was wrong for her to have gotten a new apartment without Nabal's permission. Abigail knew, though, that she could have never orchestrated this whole move if Nabal had not gone out of town. For her it was a matter of survival and protection. The Abigail in the story from 1 Samuel did kind of the same thing. She went without her Nabal's knowledge to meet David and bring him gifts. In the same way, that Abigail knew that had she gone and consulted Nabal, he would have prevented her from going.

Another church friend said to Abigail, "Gee, I know things are bad, and I know that you think you are doing the right thing, but I just can't be a part of this thing." He held up his hand, his right index finger about a quarter of an inch away from his thumb and said, "You know, I have been asking your husband to come to the men's weekly Bible study and I think he's this close to coming. If he finds out I helped you, he'll never attend." In this particular case, if you have been asking Nabal to join a Bible meeting for six months and he has never shown up, chances are that he never will. These comments show Abigail that you are not concerned about her safety. Remember, this is Nabal's wake up call. When he gets back from California and sees that his wife has moved out, this may be what it takes for him to change.

Well, the move is only part of the surprise. Abigail has also gone to an attorney, and when Nabal returns he is going to be promptly served with divorce papers. A church leader asked her about this and she said, "I have no choice. Unless there is a court order spelling out visitation rights for our daughter, he could come back, take my daughter from pre-school and never return her to me." "Well, you know, the Bible says that you cannot get a divorce, unless you want to be guilty of adultery," the church leader tells her.

Yet, another Abigail comes to church, her husband used to, but he has drifted off into heavy alcohol and drug usage. When he is drunk or high, he becomes very violent. He hits his wife and even throws things at their kids. This Nabal will chase his wife around the house, corner her in the kitchen and then punch and slap her. One night, Abigail is backed into a corner and she knows what is coming next, so she pushes him back just as he is about to slap her. Abigail tells her elder about this and he says to her, "You have to turn the other cheek, Jesus said so, you can't hit back or push." This is bad advice. Every state in the country allows for self-defense. Is a woman who is being strangled supposed to just stand there and let her abuser kill her? Is a victim supposed to just sit there and let an abuser knock her teeth out? Victims can tell you when they are about to be assaulted. Most victims that I have dealt with have felt the altercation brewing for weeks or days or hours. Remember, the victim's safety is at risk. Don't try to tell Abigail that she cannot protect herself. Who knows, this could be the night that she will be critically injured or killed.

This same Abigail decided that enough was enough, so she poured out every bottle of brandy, whiskey and every can of beer. She also flushed Nabal's marijuana down the toilet. Nabal woke up and saw what she had done and he went ballistic. Nabal grabbed her hair, dragged her around the house, kicked her, punched her, and one of their children called 9-1-1. The police arrived and arrested Nabal, who even fought with them. At the jail, Nabal called Abigail collect and screamed at her, vowing to kill her after his release. Nabal had several felony charges, and a court commissioner ordered that he have no contact with his wife and that he could not consume alcohol or drugs. This Nabal defied every order that was handed down and went to a tavern right after his release. After he was highly intoxicated, he confronted Abigail at home and was now-re-arrested for bail jumping. You see, the first arrest was his wake up call, and we can see what he chose to do with that. Had he been contrite and willing to change, things may have been different.

Abigail goes to church that Sunday and tells the church leaders what had happened. Everyone tells her how proud they were that she took a stand and followed through with a report. During the next week, Nabal is stalking her and will not obey the court orders. He is arrested again, and the next Sunday Abigail tells the church leaders what a great help the local domestic violence advocacy agency has been. "They have even offered me reduced fees for an attorney," Abigail tells them. "Wait a minute," one church leader says, "an attorney for what?" Abigail says, "For a divorce." The church leader then tells her that this is moving too fast and that she cannot get a divorce. He says, "Well, you know, divorce is the unpardonable sin."

The only "unpardonable sin" that is listed in the Bible is referenced in Mark 3:29 where Jesus says, "But whoever blasphemes against the Holy Spirit will never be forgiven; he is guilty of an eternal sin," (NIV). The Pharisees were confronting Jesus who had been driving demons out of people. The Pharisees, in trying to discredit Jesus, were saying that Jesus was possessed by "Beelzebub" and said in verse 22 of that same chapter: "By the prince of demons he is driving out demons," (NIV). The Pharisees were trying to say that Jesus had an evil spirit in him. Jesus was saying that anyone who slanders the work and the person of the Holy Spirit gives up redemption and salvation. Never did Jesus ever say that divorce was the unpardonable sin. I know of one church in particular that teaches this, and the amazing thing is that I know some men who have been divorced after 5, 10 and 25 years of marriage, and when they want to re-marry, a simple donation of $3,000 to the home office of that church granted them an annulment. So, let's stop telling Abigail that she is going to be guilty of an "unpardonable sin." To do such is modern day legalism, in my opinion.

Now, another church leader told this same Abigail that she could not get a divorce because of Jesus' teaching found in Matthew Chapter 19. Let's look at this, and the best place to start is to see where Jesus had just come from in Chapter 18. Jesus had just ended his Galilean ministry and was now moving on to his Perean ministry. It is just months before he will be crucified, and right away, after crossing the Jordan as he enters Judea, the Pharisees are there waiting to discredit Jesus and to find some way to stop him or destroy him. And they pick this topic of divorce to "test" Jesus. They want to end his ministry now, but Jesus knows that it can't end now, that everything has to go as planned by his Father in Heaven.

The Pharisees also pick the topic of divorce at this location because of where he is. Jesus is in the land of Herod Antipas who has already had John the Baptist beheaded for his teachings on divorce, so the Pharisees hope to make Jesus give some harsh discourse on divorce so that Herod will have a reason to arrest and kill him.

So Jesus chooses his words carefully and first reminds them from Genesis 1:27 that God created a man and a woman, in the beginning and that they were made for each other, not for anyone else who came along. This shifted the opinions of Jesus to the word of God, which the Pharisees believed and followed. So the Pharisees ask Jesus, why did Moses command a certificate of divorce to allow one to divorce his wife? Jesus answers by saying that Moses did allow divorce in a case of adultery, and he says that Moses permitted divorce because their hearts were hard towards their wives. Jesus simply reiterated what Moses had said because of the crowds following him, and even the Pharisees were all trying to live up to the laws handed down by Moses. In the days of Moses, husbands could receive a certificate of divorce for any reason. We know this because, had the wife been caught in adultery, she would have been killed, because the punishment for adultery was death. And these women were not being killed, they were sent off, for whatever reason. Maybe he didn't like how she cooked, or maybe she bore him only daughters and he wanted sons in order to carry on his name. It's also interesting that the women were never allowed to divorce, so the command was given to men and Jesus was talking to men.

And Nabal, the church leader, who shows the church his nice side but is very nasty and violent at home, will stand over Abigail, with his Bible open, and he will pound his finger into the Book of Matthew and tell Abigail that if she gets a divorce from him she will send herself into adultery.

But there is more in the Bible about divorce than what is covered in Matthew. We read in 1 Corinthians Chapter 7 as the Apostle Paul writes back to the church in Corinth about the topic of marriage. First off, Paul says in verse 12: "To the rest I say this (I not the Lord)," (NIV), and what he is saying is that he speaks for Jesus here – that what he is about to say has the same validity as the words of Jesus (and, after all, were not all men and women who wrote the Bible writing the instructions of God through the Holy Spirit?) And to understand what Paul is about to say about divorce, look at the people he is talking to. He is writing to the church of Corinth. Unlike the Jews that Jesus spoke to, the City of Corinth was a wicked, vial place. No one there was trying to live up to the laws of Moses or God. Even when one referred to a person of Corinth, the very name of the city meant lascivious, lewd and wicked. Corinth was a pagan place and their worship, before Paul's teachings, involved all kinds of perverse acts.

So Paul introduces these wicked and sinful people to the Gospel, and right away the new converts start asking questions of Paul, which prompted his answers. What were the questions? Read his answers and you can figure out what their questions were. They asked him what should a new believer do if his or her spouse does not become a believer – should we divorce? And Paul says in verses 12-14, "If any brother has a wife who is not a believer and she is willing to live with him, he must not divorce her. And if a woman has a husband who is not a believer and he is willing to live with her, she must not divorce him. For the unbelieving husband has been sanctified through his wife, and the unbelieving wife has been sanctified through her believing husband," (NIV).

But Paul goes on to say in verse 15 of Chapter 7: "But if the unbeliever leaves, let him do so. A believing man or woman is not bound in such circumstances; God has called us to live in peace," (NIV). So if Nabal is a pastor, or an elder, a deacon or a Sunday school teacher, and he claims to be a believer, is he really a believer if he is verbally, emotionally, physically or sexually abusing his wife? If Nabal, the church leader, tells Abigail that he is going on vacation for two weeks because "God told me to," and that during that time he will decide whether they will stay together or Abigail will have to leave the house and kids, could he really be a believer? Especially after all that we have studied, from God's word about what love is, and what the duties of a husband are?

So, let's quit telling Abigail that she cannot divorce. Again, restoration is the ultimate goal, but it is up to Nabal to make some changes and to work on the marriage. Instead of preaching to Abigail about why she cannot seek a divorce, especially when her safety is at risk, is wrong. Nabal should instead be confronted as to why he is not trying to make the home a peaceful place.

Some church leaders will tell Abigail that Malachi 2:16 says that "God hates divorce." But church leaders leave out the rest of the verse which reads: "And I hate a man's covering himself with violence as well as with his garment," (NIV). God is talking to men, who in verse 15, "Because the Lord has been a witness between you and the wife of your youth, with whom you have dealt treacherously; yet she is your companion," (NKJV). So while, yes, God hates divorce, sometimes if the choice is for the woman to stay in the abusive relationship or leave, fleeing to safety is the better option. Instead of telling Abigail, "God hates divorce," let's ask Nabal, "Why do you cover yourself with violence?" which God also hates.

Some say that it is too hard to predict whether or not a victim would end up a homicide statistic, but it really isn't that difficult to figure out at all. We need to believe Abigail, we need to get a real sense of the fear that she has in staying in close contact with her abuser. If she can answer "yes" to any of the following questions, she is indeed at great risk of great bodily harm, even death:

Have you ever been injured?

Has there been more than one incident of physical violence?

Have you ever suffered physical pain from an incident?

Have you ever sought medical treatment?

Do you fear that the abuser will continue to harm you?

Do you believe that your abuser is capable of killing you?

Have you ever been strangled?

Does the abuser use alcohol or drugs on a regular basis?

Have the children ever been injured?

Has the abuser ever harmed or killed a family pet?

Has the abuser ever threatened to harm or kill a pet?

Does the abuser keep track of your daily routine?

Has the abuser ever threatened to kill you?

Has the abuser ever made threats to kill himself/herself?

Has the abuser actually carried out an act to attempt to kill himself/herself?

The answers to these questions are the best predictor of what could happen to the victim, and any affirmative answer to any of these questions are huge indicators that some intervention needs to take place.

I know a woman who asked a Christian counselor if she should divorce her abusive husband. The counselor told her that she should separate to try to get him to see his abusive tendencies and get him to deal with his abusive behavior. The counselor told her to work at saving the marriage and to stay away until the husband changed his ways.

Another Christian counselor told another woman that through tough love she should leave the abusive home, never divorce and after making it clear that she would not return until the abuse ended, wait, if it takes a year or three years or eight years. If he never responds, never return, but do not divorce.

Now, don't get me wrong, I really believe that reconciliation through change is what the goal here should be. However, unless the victim is independently wealthy and the couple has no kids, the advice given by the counselors will never work.

Abusers know that domestic violence shelters cannot house victims, in most cases, more than 30 to 60 days. There comes a point when the shelter has to make room for new victims. The victim has a home where she could live, if the abuse would end or if Nabal would leave. But Nabal will not leave. Nabal will withhold funds from Abigail. Nabal will sneak over to the school and take the kids and not allow her to visit them.

In the real world, and in a majority of cases, Abigail is not wealthy and cannot hold out and wait a year, three years or eight years. Nabal will refuse to make the house payment. Both will lose all of the equity in the home.

Abigail will have to take legal action to protect her financial interests in the home. Nabal will come and take her car from her work parking lot. And since their names are both on the title, he can do that. Abigail will need a judge to intervene and tell Nabal that he must give up her car.

A judge will have to set up visitation and placement of the children. Yes, divorce is devastating on kids, but so is constantly being fought over, used as pawns, and being that evening with whichever parent happened to get to the daycare or school before the other one did. So, while divorce is and should be the last resort, we need to open our eyes or open our wallets and be prepared to give Abigail tens of thousands of dollars and more to not proceed with a divorce, because that is what it will take.

Nabal will sit back and wait. He will wait for the shelter to say, "Time's up, you have to leave." He will wait for Abigail's parents or sister or brother-in-law to say, "Gee, Abigail, you have been here six months, we just can't have you here any longer." And, because Nabal knows these things will happen, he can sit back and wait, and he will take her back, but on his terms, and Abigail is right back in the abusive situation that she left. Nabal wins, Abigail loses, and all at the advice of Christian people whom Abigail trusted and listened to. And, once Abigail leaves and has to return to the abuser, how easy do you think it will be for her to ever try to break away again?

Do not tell the victim that she MUST get a restraining order. Many women who have applied for restraining orders have ended up killed by their abuser. The abuser gets very irate when the victim applies for a restraining order because the abuser knows that this was an action that the victim sought. If an arrest is made and the court system imposes a no contact order, the abuser will still be angry, but most of the anger will be directed at the court system rather than at Abigail. There are cases where a restraining order is a good idea. But it is still best to give Abigail all of her options and to let an advocate from the domestic violence agency work through these issues with her.

If Abigail and Nabal do separate and a divorce is pursued, Abigail will need plenty of help caring for the children. Nabal, in most cases, will refuse to take the kids on any other days than the court-appointed visitation times. Abigail will also need emotional support because Nabal will fight her all the way and make the division of property and other issues next to impossible to resolve. Nabal will also talk badly of Abigail to the children, and he will tell the children that all of this is "mommy's fault."

I was listening to Dr. Tony Evans of the radio program "The Urban Alternative" one day, and he had a special message for the single people in the church. He was trying to encourage them, as many single people wonder how long they will go on without finding someone to date or marry. Dr. Evans was telling them to continue to pray and trust that God would bring the right person into their lives. In his sermon, Dr. Evans made a very wise comment. He said that the worst thing than going through life single is to be married to the wrong person. I can tell you that from working with families in the church, and also on the streets as a cop, no truer words could be spoken.

For that reason, I would strongly suggest to single people that when they feel they have met Mr. or Mrs. Right, they need to do some investigating to make sure that this person is right for them. I have counseled people to hire a private investigator to have a background check done. In Wisconsin, you can check at www.wisconsincircuit courtaccess.com to check circuit court arrest records. If the person that you are about to marry has arrests and convictions for battery, criminal damage to property or disorderly conduct, these are huge red flags and you need to stop, slow things down and look into these cases. Remember, the best predictor of future behavior is past behavior.

If Abigail returns to Nabal, and there has been no change, and she is still in an abusive situation, do not judge her or tell her, "Why don't you leave?" or, "Haven't you had enough?" Remember that there are many complex issues here, financial considerations and fear that the children will be taken away by the abuser. Just stay in touch with Abigail and continue to be supportive.

If Abigail is not ready to make such a move or fears the consequences of moving out right now, do not force her or tell her that she must. Any intervention into a violent marriage must honor and respect the wishes of the victim. Abigail may need more time and more counsel. Just continue to be a source of support for her and encourage her to meet with the Domestic Abuse and Sexual Assault advocacy agencies. Your church could set up a weekly meeting between these advocates and Abigail and encourage them to meet in a room at the church. Abigail's husband may be following her and may become violent if he finds out that she is going to the offices of the local abuse agency. This is why you should encourage these support meetings to take place during the week at the church. She will feel better, too, because she doesn't have to lie to Nabal about where she is going. She can tell him that she has a meeting at church to attend and be truthful at the same time.

One last comment about restraining orders: sometimes police officers or those trying to intervene on Abigail's behalf will tell her to seek an order of protection. These people may really feel that this is the route she should go, while others, it's almost as though they are telling Abigail, "O.K., if you are serious about changing your circumstances, then do something to prove it." Oftentimes, people hear of a murder/ suicide case involving Intimate Partners and they call this a "crime of passion," and they try to understand the crime by saying that the abuser and victim were arguing and the abuser lost control over his actions. There is nothing passionate about murder or suicide, and I can tell you that from the thousands of domestic abuse cases that I have handled, or reviewed, it is highly unlikely that the abuser just "snapped" and then killed his wife. While we cannot ask these dead victims what happened in the last few minutes of their lives, it is my opinion that the victim had just announced that she was moving out or filing for a divorce. What triggered the homicide and subsequent suicide was not Nabal losing control of himself but, rather, Nabal saw that he was about to lose control over Abigail. Abusers love control and anything or anyone who takes away that control serves as a threat to a Nabal.

We must all realize that an order of protection is just a piece of paper, and that piece of paper must be accompanied with a safety plan and an unknown location for Abigail. When the victim applies for a restraining order, her name is on that paperwork, along with her handwritten story which outlines why she seeks protection, and her signature appears at the bottom of the page. When Nabal reads this, he will be totally enraged that the very person he has been controlling has now turned the tables on him and is now seeking, through the courts, the ability to control him. I have heard many irate men say, "How dare she!!" or, "This means war!!" The question then is how long can Abigail stay in hiding? She will have to go to work at some point. She will have to have some interaction with Nabal during child visitation exchanges, and there are plenty of women who have been murdered many months after the initial hearing for the protection order. Abigail needs wisdom and guidance through this decision, and the experts, I believe, are the advocates at the domestic abuse and sexual assault programs in your community.

Well, I hope that you have a better understanding of abuse and just how dangerous domestic violence is. We need to put the safety and care of the victim and children first, and this takes a lot of time and money. The next time you are aware of a domestic violence situation, in or outside of your church, I hope that you take the situation seriously and help the victim and the abuser see that what is happening is wrong and plan out a successful intervention.

If you have any comments or questions, you can always feel free to e-mail me at: www.squadtalk@msn.com. And above all, remember, Nothing Changes if Nothing Changes.

Safety Planning for Domestic Violence Victims

- If you are being physically attacked, curl up and protect your head. Teach your children to do the same thing.

- If an argument is escalating and you fear for your safety, keep the phone with you and move the argument out of the kitchen where there are knives. Try to avoid rooms where there may be guns and stay in rooms that have exit doors. If you can get to a bathroom that has a locking door, lock yourself and your children inside and dial 9-1-1 immediately.

- Know where your wallet and car keys are at all times. This will make a quick escape much easier.

- Have an escape drill with your children when the abuser is away. Figure out how everyone in the home will get out safely and where to meet outside.

- Have a code word. There was a case recently where a victim and her children were kidnapped by her husband. The victim was allowed to call her parents, and she had previously told them that should she ever say a certain word, that this would be a sign that she and her kids were in grave danger. Have a code word that your children know, so that when you say it, they know to dial 9-1-1.

- Have a safe place to go. Know how to contact the local Domestic Violence Advocacy Center/Shelter. If you go to a hotel, pay cash for the room. If the abuser calls the credit card company and requests to know where a jointly held credit card has been used recently, the abuser will know where you are. Tell the hotel clerk that you are checking in under an assumed name and ask that the hotel not disclose your name or room number to anyone without your consent. Park your car a few blocks away from the hotel. Some abusers will drive through every hotel lot in town until they find the victim's car. A close friend from church may also be an option, but plan it out ahead of time.

- Start parking your car backed into the driveway. Keep the driver's side door unlocked and the other doors locked. This will aid you in a quick escape.

- Have a suitcase handy with several changes of clothes for you and your children. Have it safely stored at a friend's or relative's house. Should your abuser discover the packed bag, your safety could be in great jeopardy.

- If you need to exchange children for visitation, tell your abuser that you will only meet him in a busy parking lot or, better yet, the parking lot of your local police department or sheriff's department.

- If you do leave, consider a post office box so you can still receive your mail.

If you do not know where the nearest Domestic Violence or Sexual Assault agencies are nearest you, please call:

National Domestic Violence Hotline
1-800-799-7233 or 1-800-787-3224 (TTY)
National Sexual Violence Resource Center

1-717-909-0710 or www.nsvrc.org

In Wisconsin:
Wisconsin Coalition Against Domestic Violence
www.wcadv.org

Wisconsin Coalition Against Sexual Assault
1-608-257-1516 or www.wcasa.org

Wisconsin Services for Elder Victims of Domestic Violence
1-608-266-2536

Wisconsin Unidos Against Domestic Violence
1-800-510-9195

Wisconsin Services for Deaf Victims of Domestic Violence
www.DHFSDeafUnity@Wisconsin.gov

LaVergne, TN USA
10 May 2010
182162LV00003B/7/P